Forms of Education

Forms of Education analyses the basic tenets of the humanist legacy in terms of its educational ethos, examining its contradictions and its limits, as well as the extent of its capture of educational thought. It develops a broader conception of educational experience, which challenges and exceeds those limits.

This book deflates the compulsion to educate. It delegitimises the imposition of any particular practice in education. It defines education, openly and non-restrictively, as the (de)formation of non-stable subjects, arguing that education does not require specific formations, nor the formation of specific forms, only that form does not cease being formed in the experience of the non-stable subject. Exploding and pluralising what amounts to 'education,' this book rethinks what might still be called educational experience against and outside the ethos of the humanist legacy that confines its meaning.

This book will be of interest to scholars and postgraduate students in the fields of philosophy of education, educational theory, history of education, and sociology of education.

Emile Bojesen is Reader in Education at the University of Winchester, UK.

Forms of Education

Rethinking Educational Experience Against and Outside the Humanist Legacy

Emile Bojesen

Routledge
Taylor & Francis Group

LONDON AND NEW YORK

First published 2020
by Routledge
2 Park Square, Milton Park, Abingdon, Oxon OX14 4RN

and by Routledge
605 Third Avenue, New York, NY 10017

First issued in paperback 2021

Routledge is an imprint of the Taylor & Francis Group, an informa business

British Library Cataloguing-in-Publication Data
A catalogue record for this book is available from the British Library

Library of Congress Cataloging-in-Publication Data
Names: Bojesen, Emile, author.
Title: Forms of education : rethinking educational experience against and outside the humanist legacy / Emile Bojesen.
Description: Abingdon, Oxon ; New York, NY : Routledge, 2020. | Includes bibliographical references and index.
Identifiers: LCCN 2019039378 (print) | LCCN 2019039379 (ebook) | ISBN 9781138481251 (hardback) | ISBN 9781351060677 (ebook)
Subjects: LCSH: Education, Humanistic. | Education--Philosophy.
Classification: LCC LC1011 .B57 2020 (print) | LCC LC1011 (ebook) | DDC 370.11/2--dc23
LC record available at https://lccn.loc.gov/2019039378
LC ebook record available at https://lccn.loc.gov/2019039379

Typeset in Bembo
by Cenveo® Publisher Services

ISBN 13: 978-1-03-208319-3 (pbk)
ISBN 13: 978-1-138-48125-1 (hbk)

Contents

Introduction

This book is a deconstruction of the humanist legacy in education. The forms of education described in this book that can be understood to partly exceed or challenge this legacy are not prescriptions intended to be imposed. Rather, they are elucidations of educational experience that often exceeds intentional education, even if they also affect and are affected by relations to it. Jettisoning all intentional or even instrumental forms of education is not the argument or aim of this book. Rejected, though, are artificially instrumental forms of education, leveraged by the social purchase of the humanist ethos and the value it affords to the 'educated person,' regardless of the individual or social significance they may have outside its constraining economy. With the dual objectives of both exploding *and* pluralising what amounts to 'education,' this book rethinks what might still be called educational experience against and outside the humanist legacy that confines its meaning. What I aim to present is support for an argument made *within* educational culture, to show how even the resources available within it unsettle the foundations and authority of imposed education. A broader conception of education offers a way to think the significance of educational experience without imposed value.

By keeping this word – education – in play, and broadening its meaning and applicability considerably, I hope to be able to show that dominant conceptions of education are absurdly limited and limiting. I reject the implication that there should be a clear, practicable notion of education, however ideal. As I go on to argue, most experiences of education are not intentional and are best conceived as the perpetual formation (and deformation) of non-stable subjects. They do not redeem experience in the name of a lofty ideal, therefore, unlike the imposed and compulsive educational practice common to the humanist legacy, they require no justification. In the context of this wider framework, this book takes a narrower focus and elucidates the educational dimensions, resonances, or implications of a selection of literary, philosophical, and psychoanalytical texts, all of which can themselves be seen as deconstructing the humanist educational legacy that might nonetheless take credit for them.

I do not only intend to challenge the dominant educational forms produced by this legacy, I also seek to forsake as beyond recuperation all alternative educational philosophies and practices that rely on its redemptive logic, wherein an original sin of educational lack is implied which can only be redeemed by a relatively specific form of education. While educational theories that explicitly perform a redemptive function require little or no mention, as they leave little to be deconstructed and demystified, more interesting and problematic are those that, in seemingly intending to avoid redemption in terms of outcome, reveal it in their very structure. That is to say, the road *to* education is very clearly paved, even if they emphasise that the point of arrival is somehow infinitely deferred or non-teleological. Whatever specific definition of education that is provided is always 'preferred,' which is to say normative.

This book does not cite many contemporary educational theorists or philosophers, primarily because they tend only to write about intentional, formal, or institutional education, usually in terms of schooling and higher education. And those who do exceed this scope are mostly concerned with 'ideal' developmental and progressive approaches to individual education, rather than being interested in educational experience as it occurs, 'ideal' or not. This book deflates rather than seeks to improve the results of the compulsion to educate, and its argument is positioned against legitimating the imposition of any practice in education, either for individuals or groups. This is not only because conceptualising ideals that should reshape the system or structure of education might well be a fool's errand or at least require the kind of revolutionary change that is beyond predictability, it is also because imposing the idea of what it means to be educated on someone else, let alone entire populations, can rightly be seen as a reprehensible and illegitimate act, even if it is now the near-global norm.

The basic logic underpinning education's imposition of values, ideals, means, and ends on to young people and societies in general is a concern barely reflected upon, even by those (such as researchers, teachers, students, parents) who are most invested in them. Instead, what comes into question most often are how the minutiae of principles and techniques in education are understood, promoted, and administered. While suggestions for practical consequences, and even possible practices, do arise throughout this book, these are not systematically determined and would best be understood as incomplete speculations developed in relation to readings of specific texts and engagement with delimited contexts. Experiences of education exceed any systematisation. Even though there are powerful themes (shared social morality; systems of accountability; rhetorics of employability, competition and social mobility) within education and society that might dictate our behaviours and even play a significant part in constructing our subjectivities, there are also other powers at work (subcultural, local, and personal interests; desires; obligations; and responsibilities) which create alternative and conflicting narratives to those which are most dominant.

Education most often occurs outside of any prescribed imposition, and descriptions of it can be generated by narratives that are much more likely to exhibit its variety than its 'truth.' For this reason I put forward a provisional definition of 'education' as *the perpetual formation (and deformation) of non-stable subjects*, to be able to frame or underpin the variety of its forms that follow. By this definition, a subject is not educated only in a linear and progressive manner but in fits and starts, by fixations and arrests, that sometimes take them in several directions at once, many of these paths being contradictory and sometimes consciously or unconsciously abandoned. My very broad definition of education is intended to imply that it can be experienced without resorting to qualifying that experience with any particular content, process, or outcome. Education is not understood here as the relative *success* of a privileged, delimited activity or experience with essential features to be learned or ends to be met. Education is not the production of a particular kind of subjectivity, or the learning of particular knowledge, dispositions, virtues, and values. Education is experienced without the requirement of verification. This is why I argue that education is most openly and non-restrictively defined as the (de)formation of non-stable subjects. It does not require specific formations, nor the formation of specific forms, only that form does not cease being formed in the experience of the non-stable subject. Such a definition of education has the capacity to include *all other definitions of education*. Equally, it does not imply that anything in particular should be done, instead laying the ground for a multitude of educational experiences to be perceived and interpreted. It also provides a ground from which to challenge the supposed legitimacy of imposed educational ideals and practices.

The approach I have taken is to select texts that help in expanding, questioning, and also deflating what it means to be an educated person. By means of reading the texts that follow in the proceeding chapters, I feel I have been able to attend to some of the complexities and nuances of forms of education that exceed those promoted in the dominant discourses and practices of intentional education. I frequently turn to literature, literary philosophy, and psychoanalytic writing in helping me to make my argument, not because they help to refine our use of language with reference to education but rather because, as Leo Bersani puts it, 'literature subverts *any* project of meaning in language, perhaps especially projects of precision in meaning. And it should thereby help us to resist the coercive designs more or less hidden in all such projects.'[1]

Literature, however, is not innocent or uncontaminated by the educational context it arises in and is therefore

> never merely an agent of resistance against networks of power-serving knowledge; instead it is one of that network's most seductive manifestations. It can never stand outside the oppressive manipulations of social reality and negate those manipulations by a willed alienation from history. Literature is on a continuum with those forces by which is has habitually proclaimed itself to be menaced.[2]

Literature is as much of a product and culprit of the perpetuation of the humanist legacy in education as it is a means of its critique. Like subjects educated in that tradition, literature cannot fully escape or resist its inheritances or contaminations. What Bersani describes also implies that the very means by which this book attempts to put the humanist educational legacy into question are themselves a product of its history, institutions, and ideologies. Literature, though, and philosophical and psychoanalytic thought that attends to it, and treats it as more than a means for a humanist education, also subverts and scuppers claims to truth, knowledge, and authenticity within the rhetoric and aesthetics of the humanist tradition.

The incredible variety of educational experiences it might be possible to chart indicates the impossibility of proclaiming some as 'authentic' and others as 'inauthentic.' The logic of authenticity, related to education and any associated politics, becomes theoretically compromised in the light of experiences that exceed, undermine, or destroy any assumed authority. What remains are approaches to education and politics that are provisionally learned and/or (often passively) decided to be believed in, for better or for worse. However, the inability to proclaim any particular approach to educational or political practice as authentic, authoritative, or true has its own educational and political implications. It does, nonetheless, not follow that because nature or philosophy do not provide a 'true' form of education or politics, we should then not prescribe anything at all. Given that education and politics will continue to affect lives regardless of what is believed, such a position would itself be a 'passive' endorsement of imposed prescriptions, many of which are accepted as self-evidently good. This kind of 'pretend escape' from ideological compromise in already contaminated milieus is not what is proposed in the chapters that follow. Equally, as the elaboration of the variety of possible educational experiences in this book hopes to show, educational experience, for better or worse, exceeds (and therefore partly resists) every aggressive claim to truth or authenticity, every sense or construct of community, and any system of forms and laws.

For Bersani, 'The social function of literature – its critical power – consists in its demystifying the force of argument, argument's claim to truth.'[3] This emphasis on demystification is also the reason for choosing to work with 'deconstructive' rather than system building thinkers. Deconstruction, in Jean-François Lyotard's understanding,

> is a truly radical critical activity for it does not deal with the *signifieds* of things, but with their plastic organization, their signifying organization. It shows that the problem is not so much that of knowing what a given discourse says, but rather how it is disposed. It shows that it is active on account of its very disposition, its configuration, and that the deconstruction of its disposition is going to reveal all of its mystifying content.[4]

The problem, therefore, is not so much that of knowing what the advocates of, and practitioners within, the humanist legacy of education say or what their arguments are, but rather in how their entire discourse is disposed in terms of its configuration, which is what underpins its institutions, its systems of accountability, actions, and so on. The dominant disposition of contemporary educational discourse and practice is marked by compulsion leveraged by the redemptive logic of the humanist legacy. The forms of education marked by this legacy can be defined as: *a particular form of education, abstracted from the majority of possible experiences, considered necessary and therefore often imposed, because subjection to its processes results in the objective improvement of its subjects and society.* What the specific content or techniques of this process are can vary and are contested, but the fundamental disposition remains the same; this *is* the humanist legacy. Clearly, such a disposition is at work in the majority of contemporary educational settings and the critical thought that attends to it, which is why it would be impossible to exhaustively determine and elucidate its innumerable manifestations. A close analysis of some of the signifiers of this disposition and their cultural effects, especially those that might superficially seem to exceed it, is the critical object of this book. Its deconstructive strategy is the resistant and antagonistic metamorphosis of educational meaning on its most prized terrain, that of 'Western intellectual culture.' The deconstructive gesture I put to work presupposes the auto-deconstructibility of the Western educational ethos; as this educational 'structure' is already heterogeneous and unstable, it is prone to destabilisation and deconstruction. By drawing on the work of Jacques Derrida, Maurice Blanchot, Sigmund Freud, Virginia Woolf, Georges Bataille, André Gide, Søren Kierkegaard, Charles Fourier, James Guillaume, Shulamith Firestone, and Ivan Illich, I intend to show how the dominant, often repressive and restricting, logic of education is wrecked most resolutely by those who might otherwise be claimed to represent its highest achievements. 'Western thought' – itself an absurd and arrogant formulation – is levied against itself.[5]

The book is divided into two distinct parts, which nonetheless frequently overlap and rely on one another. The first part, Against, which incorporates Chapters 1–5, analyses the tenets of the humanist legacy in terms of its educational ethos, examining its contradictions and its limits, as well as the extent of its capture of educational thought. The second part, Outside, which incorporates Chapters 6–10, strives to develop a broader conception of educational experience, which challenges and exceeds the limits of the humanist educational ethos.

Chapter 1 outlines the key historical, rhetorical, and aesthetic features of the humanist legacy in education and elucidates how they have come to be pervasive in education and educational thought. It traces a line from Plato in Ancient Greece, through Cicero and Quintilian in Ancient Rome, to the humanists of the European Renaissance, and towards the eighteenth and nineteenth centuries, where the civic ideologies of education took hold in the form of compulsory schooling. Using the example of the anarchist educational thinker, Herbert Read, the chapter concludes with the suggestion that even much radical educational thought is underpinned by the abstractly redemptive, hierarchically imposed, and socially stratifying and harmonising impulses and logic of the humanist legacy.

Educational disharmony and unsociability are, in Chapter 2, explored as the limit, as the adversary, but also as a resource of the logic of the humanist legacy in education. Forms of educational experience which exceed its harmonising narrative are either negatively stigmatised or become the subject of educational redemption in the name of social progress. Framed by Blanchot's analysis of culture, humanist aspects of the social and educational thought of Immanuel Kant and John Dewey are opposed to those of Søren Kierkegaard and André Gide. Kierkegaard's *Fear and Trembling* and Gide's *The Counterfeiters* are shown to both critique and offer alternatives to the humanist legacy's dominant conceptions of educational significance.

Radical political and educational ideas, Chapter 3 argues, often become domesticated through a received conception of education rooted in the humanist legacy, an argument which resonates with domestication as described by Darren Webb in the context of the domestication of utopian thought, where the 'subversive, counter-hegemonic thrust of utopia has been tamed and rendered fit for domestic life within the established order.'[6] Offering critiques of educational elements of ostensibly philosophical texts that are sometimes held up as presenting radical alternatives to contemporary education, Jacques Rancière's *The Ignorant Schoolmaster* and Dewey's *How We Think*, this chapter goes on to show how Charles Fourier's genuinely radical educational notion of integral education became domesticated by the anarchist tradition and Franciso Ferrer's Modern School. James Guillaume's anarchistic utopian thinking on education is revealed as a notable exception. More Foureirian in form, Guillaume's thought is aligned and developed alongside radical thought from the 1970s; that of Shulamith Firestone, and two of Fourier's readers, Pierre Klossowski and Italo Calvino, showing how his principles resonated with radical social and educational thought in the 1970s, and might do so again today.

Chapter 4 turns to some of the educational resonances of the thought of Georges Bataille and Maurice Blanchot. While later chapters will explore how aspects of their thought can contribute to conceiving of forms of educational experience at a distance from the humanist legacy, here more obviously critical aspects of their thought are applied. Dominant forms of educational practice are shown surreptitiously to exhibit elements of what Bataille calls productive and unproductive expenditure. Features of the more pernicious elements of education as a cultural device are then studied in Blanchot's récits (short stories), *The Idyll* and *The Last Word*, revealing how expenditure is only valued, in the dominant educational economy, inasmuch as it re-entrenches social order and, within it, already existing power and privilege.

The subject of Chapter 5 is the legitimation of the dominant contemporary educational economy, grounded in the humanist legacy, and its de-legitimation or co-option of educational forms which resist or evade its capture. Drawing on Gilles Deleuze's thoughts in *Bergsonism* – on education, and what he calls 'order-words,' the 'real,' and the 'virtual' – to be able to diagnose the structure and effect of educational legitimation, the chapter goes on to provide examples of educational practice against and outside the humanist legacy. José Medina's notion of 'resistant imagination' provides the means to think of a dominant mode of education first and foremost in terms of its injustices, and James C. Scott's reflections on 'mētis,' as a locally situated form of expertise, present an opportunity to rethink where educational legitimacy can come from and where it could, more justly, be grounded.

Chapter 6 introduces the Freudian psychoanalytic terminology that will be applied and developed in the two chapters that follow. Outlining Freud's description of the operation of the psychic economy and its relationship to educational experience, this chapter demonstrates how the dominant logic of education co-opts the libidinal energy of the id in its seizure of the often oppressive powers of the super-ego. Deleuze and Félix Guattari are also drawn upon to show how Freud's analysis of the psychic economy might itself be symptomatic of the effects of the humanist legacy in education.

A close reading of the first three sections of Woolf's novel, *The Waves*, provides the primary focus of Chapter 7. Woolf's fictional descriptions of children's educational experiences, despite – or perhaps even because of – her own ambivalent and even critical attitude towards Freud, aligns with and takes further educational aspects of the Freudian psychic economy. *The Waves* not only exemplifies the variable consequences the experience of formal education has for the children in her novel, it also gives an indication of the breadth of other forms of educational experience available to and effecting on them. The central argument of this chapter is that these broader experiences are, in fact, educational, despite not conforming to logic inherited from the humanist legacy and perpetuated in the dominant contemporary educational economy.

The now Freudian-inflected myth of Narcissus, as interpreted and developed by Blanchot and Derrida, is the subject of Chapter 8, which makes the argument that education does not have to rely on social repression, nor its concomitant psychic repressions. Moving beyond the strictures of primary and secondary narcissism, Blanchot and Derrida introduce a third form of narcissism, what Pleshette DeArmitt calls a 'narcissism of the other,' that inaugurates a self, or non-stable subject, through relation to the other. Conditioned by différance (as the possibility of the formation of form), this manner of educational relation is active in all relations between individuals, again illustrating the breadth of educational experience in excess of that which is commonly conceived within the limits of thought and practice.

Chapter 9 moves beyond the educational experiences available between individuals to those that are possible within a more general context of educational space. A broader conception of educational space does not require any of the justifications or legitimations of education in the tradition of the humanist legacy. It de-specifies the content, process, and outcome of educational experience and does not rely on the redemption of that experience in the name of an educational ideal. It substitutes the notion of a lack, that engenders the supposed moral necessity of particular and limited forms of education, for Bataille's 'principle of insufficiency,' which makes possible all forms of educational experience, regardless of their moral content. Developing, with the thought of Bataille, alongside that of Blanchot and Derrida, a notion of educational experience outside of intention, this chapter also explores how educational experiences which put things into question might be conceived in terms of what Blanchot designates as 'the limit experience.'

Blanchot's notion of conversation ('entretien') is, in Chapter 10, presented as a form of intentional but non-oppressive and non-authoritarian educational relation. Putting into question conceptions and practices of dialogue and dialectic in education, a practice of conservation as education and as educational research is developed. Conversation is a means to thinking serious and purposive educational endeavours outside the strictures of the humanist legacy and the dominant educational economy. Not reliant on linear progress or the growth of a stable subject, Blanchot's conversation opens up a path to thinking an education devoid of what he calls 'imperious monologues.'

The book concludes with a further elaboration on the educational implications of conversation, this time as understood by Jean-François Lyotard, whose thought supports in the development of a notion of educational prescription without mastery. The significant social and educational implications of this notion are gestured towards and contextualised in terms of the broader argument of the book.

Notes

1 Leo Bersani, *The Freudian Body* (New York: Columbia University Press, 1986), 67.
2 Leo Bersani, *The Culture of Redemption* (Cambridge, MA: Harvard University Press, 1990), 198.
3 Bersani, *The Freudian Body*, 67.
4 Jean-François Lyotard, *Driftworks* (New York: Semiotext(e), 1984), 29–30.
5 For a complementary example of work which challenges impositions of educational 'good' from primarily non-Western perspectives, see: Madhu Suri Prakash and Gustavo Esteva, *Escaping Education: Living and Learning within Grassroots Cultures* (New York: Peter Lang, 2008). While I find myself in agreement with their analysis, and aligned with their political disposition towards this dominant and pervasive form of education, my own book finds another locus of enquiry and attempts a different strategy. Their concern is less with regions already thoroughly contaminated by the humanist legacy in education and instead with protecting from it those regions and peoples not yet thoroughly caught in its grips. While they reveal the poverty of Western educational culture, especially when compared to what they call 'Two-Thirds World' culture, I attempt to do so from 'inside' its logic, showing how this culture deconstructs itself.
6 Darren Webb, 'Educational Studies and the Domestication of Utopia,' *British Journal of Educational Studies*, 64:4 (2016), 440.

Part I

Against

Chapter 1

Legacy

The humanist legacy

This book is less concerned with the humanist educational legacy as an object of enquiry or critique than with the elaboration of theoretical resources that might assist in evading, resisting, and, where possible, scuppering and obviating its influence. However, to make clear the stakes involved, this chapter outlines its key features as relevant to my arguments. Its disposition, as stated in the introduction, is manifested in many guises, but its fundamental traits remain the same, in that it is always manifested as a particular form of education, abstracted from the majority of possible experiences; its indispensability is, for its advocates, often unquestionable because subjection to its processes will necessarily, as far as they are concerned, result in the objective improvement of its subjects and usually also society; for this reason some of its more scalable forms are also often made compulsory.

Even beyond its more obvious historical origins in Ancient Rome, humanist education's redemptive philosophical origins go at least as far back as Plato. Adriana Cavarero shows how the myth of the cave in Plato's *Phaedo* concludes by presenting the 'philosopher's theoretically correct vertical posture,' which figures the image, in all its symbolic power, of 'the philosopher straightening up according to the perpendicular line of truth.'[1] This theme of rectitude also has moral as well as epistemological corollaries in other more explicitly educational sections of the *Republic*, where correct shaping of children's souls is discussed,[2] and where the interlocutors agree that 'the final outcome of education [...] is a single newly finished person, who is either good or the opposite.'[3] This is seen as an educational rather than legislative task, though the latter remains in play, legislating the soul. Plato also outlines the kind of person this education is intended to produce, which is 'a decent person who is most self-sufficient in living well and, above all others, has the least need of anyone else.'[4] This sets the tone for the kind of posture that is at the heart of most formal education in the West. Plato's self-sufficient person, who has the least need of anyone else, and is nonetheless subservient to the interests of the state as a good citizen and cognisant of social and educational hierarchies (as implied by the *Republic*'s social order), could be updated to describe what is desired in contemporary mass education, at least in as far as successive government and much institutional policy is concerned.

Despite this seemingly clear line straight from Plato to the present, the educationally informed posture of rectitude was most influentially developed later in Ancient Rome, first by Cicero and then by Quintilian, both of whom were central to humanist education from its earliest manifestations in fifteenth-century Italy. As Margo Todd shows, this was as much of a practical development as it was a result of ideological influence:

> The demand for practical moral and ethical instruction in both grammar schools and universities gave rise to a 'textbook revolution' consisting in a revived use of ancient moralists and an enthusiastic adoption of new humanist textbooks. The most admired classical writers were used both as pedagogical guides and as instructors in virtuous behaviour. Plutarch's treatise on the upbringing of children (first translated from Greek by Guarino in 1411). Quintilian's *Education of the Orator* (first published in full by Poggio in 1417), and Cicero's *De Oratore* (rediscovered in 1422) were among the most popular of the dual purpose manuals.[5]

Their rhetorical posturing was practical and symbolic, and, although predominantly focused on performance and persuasion, was also – at least in theory – seen as a means to developing a socially active, morally good persona. While both Cicero and Quintilian are wary of the possible abuse of eloquent oratory, their engagement with that problem only stretches as far as a few pages. Notably in Cicero's *De Oratore*[6] and *De Inventione*, where, in the latter, he states that 'men ought none the less to devote themselves to the study of eloquence although some misuse it both in private and in public affairs.'[7] And while Quintilian, in his *Institutio Oratoria*, argued that the perfect orator could 'not exist except in the person of a good man'[8] he goes on to state that while they should 'be the sort of man who can truly be called "wise," not only perfect in morals [...] but also in knowledge and in his general capacity for speaking. Such a person has perhaps never existed; but that is no reason for relaxing our efforts to attain this ideal.'[9] Thus, if students were, predictably, unable to attain sufficient moral and epistemological rectitude, they should at least be able to attain the posture which suggests it. The majority of their rhetorical texts, and certainly the aspects of their texts that were taken up in the Renaissance, were explicitly dedicated to rhetorical practice qua practice rather than relational responsibility, precisely because it was assumed that a concentration on the former would best guide and serve the ends of the latter.

In a sense, Plato's notions of the proper deportment of the soul and the models of Renaissance humanism have been inherited as superstitions which frame particular, but extremely widely practiced and understood, conceptions of learning. Despite the origins of humanism in the *studia humanitatis* of classical antiquity, preoccupied with activities 'including grammar, rhetoric, history, poetry, and moral philosophy,' as Donald R. Kelly puts it, in the Renaissance (perhaps echoing a phase of its imperial Roman history) it became 'an imperialistic as well as a revolutionary movement.'[10] The humanists of the Renaissance 'went beyond their ancient models in appreciating the deeper implications and potentials of the *studia humanitatis*.'[11] The development of Renaissance humanism was responding to the 'needs and aspirations of a secular, commercial, expanding urban society that most directly promoted the arts of communication and, in this connection, literacy, literature, and their attendant cultural attitudes.'[12] Writing specifically on the English history of humanism, Todd pinpoints education as central to its mission and its impact, arguing that

> If a single area of reform can be isolated as that in which Christian humanists had their greatest effect on sixteenth century English society, that area would be education. In their authorship of new pedagogical theory and in their participation in concrete reforms, they acted upon their conviction that a good education is the best means to combat social evil. Sin, they argued, springs at least partly from false opinions; therefore education is requisite for the installation of virtue, whether individual or social.[13]

As much, though, as this form of education was developed to combat social evil, it was also intended to develop sensibilities. Anthony Grafton and Lisa Jardine are clearer than Kelly and Todd on the elitist and hierarchical impositions this development facilitated, arguing that

> The older system [scholasticism] had fitted perfectly the needs of the Europe of the high middle ages, with its communes, its church offices open to the low-born of high talents and its vigorous debates on power and authority in state and church. The new system, we would argue, fitted the needs of the new Europe that was taking shape, with its closed governing élites, hereditary offices and strenuous efforts to close off debate on vital political and social questions. It stamped the more prominent members of the new élite with an indelible cultural seal of superiority, it equipped lesser members with fluency and the learned habit of attention to detail and it offered everyone a model of true culture as something given, absolute, to be mastered, not questioned – and thus fostered in all its initiates a properly docile attitude towards authority.[14]

This 'indelible cultural seal of superiority' operates as a form of social signalling, still conveyed today by those who attend prestigious schools or universities, where the 'content' of the learning is secondary to the social cipher it produces as a means of recognising an individual's higher status. The cipher is not empty, though, as it requires validation through assumptions about the type and quality of education received, ensuring its value as social currency.

The imprint of this seal has been exponentially multiplied and expanded through the advent of compulsory public education and can be found even in the most democratic and emancipatory approaches to education. It implies an original sin of educational lack that only education can redeem. The implication of this lack in its subjects obscures the lack at the core of its mission. Unlike the delimited form of education promoted by Renaissance humanists, who were clear and forthright about their mission, contemporary education in keeping with the humanist legacy not only obscures its origins but also their purposiveness. For the most part, the necessity of the imposition of compulsory education is no longer in question. As Ansgar Allen and Roy Goddard put it:

> Reliant as it is on modern humanism that can only justify itself by reference to its unplumbed depths, modern education is cast adrift, and hence left uncertain of its mission and purpose. It can only grasp on to the one thing it knows to be certain, which is itself, its own practices and procedures. Almost all that remains of education, then, is the reality of its existing techniques and methods. Consequently, these techniques and methods are held very close indeed. One might say, they are the 'heart and soul' of education today.[15]

The dilution of the mission and purpose of humanist education provide ample resource for educational philosophers, theorists, and activists, as well as those simply disappointed in contemporary education, to make stands for a return to something like its founding principles, often updated to be aligned with the latest philosophical or psychological trends. This step back from the emptiness of 'techniques and methods' (nonetheless always implying particular techniques and methods) cannot avoid the hierarchical, redemptive logic extant in the origins of humanist education.

The rhetorical posture figured in the works of Cicero and Quintilian represents a performative moral rectitude, while making sure to display its authenticity, as well as the authenticity of the education that has provided it. The false logic of the relationship, between performative wisdom and authority through eloquence to moral goodness, persists to this day. The sense also pervades that good education (whatever that might be represented as in whatever instance) is not only edificatory but also easily perceivable; usually through which school and university were attended and which subject was studied and what grades conferred, and also often through the accent, vocabulary, and manners of the individuals, which is to say, their rhetorical disposition. The experience and personal consequences of the education received often only matter in terms of how they can be presented, either through ones' actions or ones' certificates and curriculum vitae.

As Kelly argues, 'In a very general sense Renaissance humanism was a form of civic ideology, and it never lost these birthmarks.'[16] This civic ideology was, in the name of the educational development of individuals' virtue, elitist, hierarchical, and implemented precisely to legitimate the control of large populations:

> From fifteenth-century Italy to late-sixteenth-century England, wherever humanist educators set about providing further education for a minority of the population, the goals of that education were set as Cicero had defined them: the production of a small, politically active minority who were heirs to a mature foreign culture, and who were thereby (it is claimed) hallmarked as of the requisite moral and intellectual calibre to make substantial contributions to their own developing communities.[17]

This immense influence of the humanist logic of education as a means to moral and intellectual betterment and signifiable superiority precipitated a cultural shift, foreshadowing a way of thinking about education and culture that continues to return, re-inform, and underpin educational thought and practice. Tracing a further shift in this direction, from the eighteenth-century Romanticism of Friedrich Schiller, through modern criticism, to the modern school, Ian Hunter explains:

> Culture ceased to be a leisurely nurturing of faculties already given in an unproblematic human nature: a nurturing typified in the formation of 'clear and distinct ideas' of the rules of taste. Redeployed as a means of reconciling his divided ethical being, culture imposed an ethical obligation on the individual to conduct himself in a certain way. Culture became the site of a specific mode of ethical subjectification. And human nature was no longer the starting point of culture, but its indefinitely deferred goal. It became a telos for a practice of the self which could never be concluded, because the kind of ethical being one aspired to become receded before each step of the dialectic of culture: each step revealing a new imbalance and a new beginning.[18]

The 'educated person,' then, becomes both highly visible as a cultural entity but also indefinitely deferred, and therefore also deferential to those who seem, thanks to their signifiable status, more educated and therefore superior. Of course the educated person has to buy in, consciously or not, to this educational logic for it to work (or, of course, be educated into it), and there are also plenty of other signifiers of superiority that are mixed in with educational superiority, such as wealth and hereditary status, for example. However, these other signifiers of superiority almost always overlap with signifiers of educational experience. It is no coincidence that there is a direct correlation between wealth and the 'quality' of education one is likely to have received, which is to say, its cultural status. However, as Hunter's focus implies, what is of even greater significance in educational logic is not, as Grafton and Jardine point out, its confirmation of the superiority of those who already have access to power and resource, but rather the part this inaugural attribute plays in the broader economy of contemporary education of mass populations. By ensuring that the school and the university are conceived of as the primary sites where education occurs, and by stratifying and hierarchising those institutions, one is able to 'complete' ones' education, up to the level of a doctorate, for example, and still be subject to two educational exigencies. The first remains institutional and exists primarily in the guise of university research, which implies that there is always more to know and knowing more is inherently valuable. The second is the inter-institutional hierarchy of education, meaning that those 'trained' in lower ranking institutions are themselves ranked lower in terms of their status as an educated person. Equally remarkable is the homogeneity of conduct and even 'style' expected of the educated person. The learned performance of the educated person is part and parcel of their ethical subjectification and imbues them with the ability to navigate and be received by this educational economy and an education-saturated culture, of course with an increasing number of caveats for those who signify as being closer to the lower end of the hierarchy.

With the introduction of compulsory schooling, more recently with the addition of quasi-compulsory higher education, the hierarchical component of education has hardly disappeared. To the contrary, it has come to incorporate large swathes of national populations around the world in its increasingly broadening stratifications. Operating, on the one hand, as a means of imposing and calculating social statuses, and as the means of *legitimating* those impositions and calculations through educational subjectification, on the other, this humanistically inspired form of education continues to spread. The point of showing how this follows from the humanist legacy of a hierarchical and elitist conception of what it means to be an educated person is to emphasise that this is not some aberration of 'neoliberal education,' corrupting a purer notion of public education. Rather, it is the very idea of the 'educated person' as being necessarily worthy of esteem that is at fault. This is because the notion of what it means to be educated is artificially separated, both in theory and practice, from everyday lives, except in the sense that it distorts and co-opts activities to suit its ends. It is primarily compartmentalised in schools and universities, as well as other state-certified institutions and professional bodies, partly by means of their effective monopoly on accrediting the educated person, as well as the compulsory and quasi-compulsory necessity of attendance at those institutions, making it seem as if education would not be possible (because it cannot be certified as 'valuable') without them. All of this when what could just as easily be called education occurs every day through individuals' own experiences, as well as relationally in families, between friends, through purposeful activity that could loosely or definitively be called work, and within and across communities.

What the humanist legacy signifies is threefold: first, that there are specific criteria involved in being considered an educated person, and that this personage is imbued with moral and social authority; second, that educators and the institutions they operate in are the primary means for the generation of such a persona; third, the humanist legacy continues to legitimate a social hierarchy of education, to which entire populations are compulsorily and quasi-compulsorily subjected. Apart from the expansion of compulsoriness,[19] all of these elements have existed in humanist education from its inception in the fifteenth century, as inherited from Ancient Rome and, to a lesser extent, Ancient Greece.

Harmony

Education, in its socially dominant form, exists to make oneself – or to be made – valuable, which implicitly means more valuable than someone else who has not been subjected to something like this form of education. In this sense, and as will be argued in Chapter 5, this form of education relies on a circular logic, whereby it legitimates and justifies itself. It can be considered a broadly 'aesthetic' education because it is not simply to do with the development of knowledge and skills, but also the development of the 'right' disposition of the individual towards the social, including a reverence for education and the educated. That disposition, or 'straightening up,' as Cavarero describes it, is one which is characterised, fundamentally, by subjection to the social logic of education itself. Ivan Illich calls this the 'hidden curriculum,' which 'necessarily conveys the message that only through schooling can an individual prepare for adulthood in society, that what is not taught in school is of little value and that what is learned outside school is not worth knowing.'[20] This process is grounded in a long-standing educational concern with shaping souls, or as Sigmund Freud might put it, successfully co-opting individual's libidinal energy in the super-ego in a manner that controls them *within* their own psychic economy.

This aesthetic educational logic, of the individual's integration into a harmonious society, also goes at least as far back as the *Republic*, where Plato's interlocutors agree that one should not 'carelessly allow the children to hear any old stories, told by just anyone, and to take beliefs into their souls that are for the most part opposite to the ones we think they should have when they are grown up.'[21] For Plato, as we have seen, the primary function of education, including the role of the arts within it, is not to convey knowledge but to shape children's souls.[22] While Plato does not advocate banishing artists or teachers from the *Republic*, he does advocate banishing the poet who tells stories which corrupt its shared moral values and that inauthentically aestheticise and abstract the asserted authenticity of its forms. Although governments, educational authorities, institutions, teachers, and individuals may not define the development of these qualities in terms of aesthetic education, historically and philosophically it is where they are at home. Aesthetic education is concerned with shaping the individual in harmony with their society, not through direct engagement with that society but through hierarchically imposed and abstracted educational means. The inheritance of this logic in contemporary education is one that is rooted significantly in the humanist legacy, where

> Reasoning along classical lines that the common weal was to be achieved not be authoritarian means, but by inculcating virtuous behaviour in the individual citizen, the Christian humanists had demanded a continuous, dynamic confrontation of the informed individual conscience with moral issues in a civic environment. The commonwealth was to be reformed from below by an emphasis on behaviour, rather than repressed from above by an insistence on obedience to prescribed outward forms. The humanist goal was a godly society, not just without disorder, but even without tension − a state in which order was guaranteed by the government of rightly informed individual conscience.[23]

Contrary to the more individualising tropes of the rhetorical education of Cicero and Quintilian, thinkers of the aesthetic aspects of public education since Plato tend to agree that its function is the education of individuals (as citizens) in prescribed conceptions and concomitant dispositions of social value. Traditionally, aesthetic education has been conceived in terms of the expedient myths of social progress and harmony, commonality and moral good, and the designation of an educational hierarchy based on one's level in and perceived standard of such an education. But its expansion in modernity has created a shift of emphasis towards individualisation, where independence, autonomy, and competitiveness have become at least as important as a more explicit ideological commonality. Education has been 'largely emptied of commitment to a singular value system or divine sanction. It is filled up instead with a variety of techniques, each justified in their own idiosyncratic way.'[24] Education's role in the social order, though, despite its variety, is underpinned by a basic logic of imposed social harmony, where education is, in principle, positioned as both the means and the achievement of that harmony. Commonality now exists not only in shared conformity to relatively conservative social values but also to the values of global capital, which superficially emphasises themes such as deregulation and freedom, while regulating that very deregulation through the logic of the imposed values of the state. The ability to exhibit an education in accordance with these values is itself valuable. This is where the rhetorical and the aesthetic meet.

Rather than pointing towards more obviously conservative or liberal conceptions of aesthetic education, which transparently exhibit these features, it is perhaps more worthwhile to point out how reverence for a humanist conception of education, which fits hand in glove with the social and philosophical history of aesthetic education, exists even for more radical thinkers. The anarchist, Herbert Read, proponent of *Education Through Art*, suggested that aesthetic education's purpose should be the evolution of a 'discipline' or the realisation and following of set 'laws of beauty.'[25] Read rejects what he thinks of as Kierkegaardian perspectives on art and education, because of their emphasis on singularity, and instead finds his precedents in both Plato and Schiller. For these two philosophers, a harmony or totality of the State, Nature, and the Individual is the ideal outcome of education. This jars remarkably with the suggestion that Read's *Education Through Art* was an attempt to promote an anarchist education in disguise, devising 'a mode of education that is in fact a method of creating anarchists by stealth.'[26] In his essay, 'The Philosophy of Anarchism,' Read minimises or is ignorant of the extent of the specific hierarchical motivations underpinning the introduction of humanist education (both in its Ancient and Renaissance forms), even going so far as to relativise the bedrock of slavery in Ancient Greek society to mark it as 'an age of political liberation' and referring to the age of the European Renaissance as an 'age of liberation' despite it being a period of near unparalleled expansion of state power, both internally and externally through colonisation. Similar elisions are of course omnipresent in contemporary educational discourse. In Read's own words:

> The great age of Greek civilization is the age of the great personalities of Greek poetry, Greek art and Greek oratory: and in spite of the institution of slavery, it can be described, relatively to the ages which preceded it, as an age of political liberation. But nearer our time we have the so-called Renaissance, inspired by this earlier Hellenic civilization, and even more conscious of the value of free individual development. The European Renaissance is an age of political confusion; but in spite of tyrannies and oppression, there is no doubt that compared with the previous period, it also was an age of liberation. The individual once more comes into his own, and the arts are cultivated and appreciated as never before. But still more significantly, there arises a consciousness of the very fact that the value of a civilization is dependent on the freedom and variety of the individuals composing it.[27]

The humanist legacy, for Read, has been a means of gradually moving towards individual liberation through education, aided (no doubt problematically in his eyes) by the progressive development of the state and its internal and colonial power. There is, then, a very basic contradiction underpinning Read's position. On the one hand, he believes that 'Creeds and castes, and all forms of intellectual and emotional grouping, belong to the past.'[28] But on the other hand, he has 'not the slightest doubt that this form of individuation represents a higher stage in the evolution of mankind.'[29] Both cannot be true. To claim that what is, to all intents and purposes, a humanist education, is the means by which mankind has reached a higher stage of evolution implies, at the very least, intellectual grouping, and by dint of such, also a designation of more or less 'evolved' castes.

Read follows Plato's understanding in the *Republic* that the child is understood as being 'most malleable and takes on any pattern one wishes to impress on it.'[30] Echoing Plato's position, Read states that 'the general purpose of education is to foster the growth of what is individual in each human being, at the same time harmonizing the individuality thus educed with the organic unity of the social group to which the individual belongs.'[31] In doing so he consciously ties himself to what he considers a Platonic and Schillerian tradition of aesthetic education. Schiller himself wrote that '[t]aste alone brings harmony into society, because it establishes harmony in the individual … All other forms of communication divide society … only communication of the beautiful unites society, because it relates what is common to them all … It is only the Beautiful that we enjoy at the same time as individual and as race, that is, as *representatives* of the race.'[32] This universal, harmonious, common, and humanistically specific conception of the aesthetic as the beautiful reveals it as that which joins the universal and, in particular, the social with the individual. Equally, for Read, 'individuality' and 'difference' are also a form of particularity within an organic social unity (which would ideally be harmonious) rather than indicative of experiential singularity (which would not be thought primarily in terms of harmony). Following his logic reveals that a humanist education is the means by which mankind can be sufficiently individualised and thereby also harmonised with a social whole.

Notes

1   Adriana Cavarero, *Inclinations: A Critique of Rectitude,* trans. Amanda Minervini and Adam Sitze (Stanford, CA: Stanford University Press, 2016), 54.
2   Plato, *Republic*, in *Plato: Complete Works*, ed. J. M. Cooper (Cambridge: Hackett, 1997), 377a–c.
3   Ibid., 425c.
4   Ibid., 387d–e.
5   Margo Todd, *Christian Humanism and the Puritan Order* (Cambridge: Cambridge University Press, 1987), 47.
6   Cicero, *De Oratore*, trans. H. Rackham (Cambridge, MA: Harvard University Press, 1942), 3.66–68.
7   Cicero, *De Inventione,* trans. H.M. Hubbell (Cambridge, MA: Harvard University Press, 1949), 1.3.4
8   Quintilian, *Institutio Oratoria*, trans. Donald A. Russell (Cambridge, MA: Harvard University Press, 2001), 57.
9   Ibid., 57.
10   Donald R. Kelly, *Renaissance Humanism* (Boston, MA: Twayne Publishers, 1991), 74.
11   Ibid., 76.
12   Ibid., 4.

13 Todd, *Christian Humanism and the Puritan Order,* 43–44.

14 Anthony Grafton and Lisa Jardine, *From Humanism to the Humanities* (Cambridge, MA: Harvard University Press, 1986), xiv.

15 Ansgar Allen and Roy Goddard, *Education and Philosophy: An Introduction* (London: Sage, 2017), 134.

16 Kelly, *Renaissance Humanism,* 4.

17 Grafton and Jardine, *From Humanism to the Humanities,* 220.

18 Ian Hunter, *Culture and Government* (Basingstoke: Macmillan, 1988), 210.

19 Murray Rothbard, *Education: Free and Compulsory* (Auburn, AL: Ludwig von Mises Institute, 1999), 19–55.

20 Ivan Illich 'In Lieu of Education,' in Ivan Illich, *Towards a History of Needs* (New York: Harper & Row, 1978), 70.

21 Plato *Republic,* 377b.

22 Ibid., 377c.

23 Todd, *Christian Humanism and the Puritan Order,* 178.

24 Allen and Goddard, *Education and Philosophy,* 134.

25 Herbert Read, *Education Through Art* (London: Faber and Faber, 1958), 283–284.

26 George Woodcock, 'The Anarchists: A Bibliographical Supplement,' in *The Anarchist Reader,* ed. George Woodcock (Glasgow: Fontana, 1977), 379.

27 Herbert Read. 'The Philosophy of Anarchism,' *The Anarchist Library.* https://theanarchistlibrary.org/library/herbert-read-the-philosophy-of-anarchism (accessed July 11, 2019), unpaginated.

28 Ibid., unpaginated.

29 Ibid., unpaginated.

30 Plato, *Republic,* 377a-b.

31 Read, *Education Through Art,* 8.

32 Friedrich Schiller, *On the Aesthetic Education of Man,* trans. R. Snell (New York: Dover, 2004), 138.

Chapter 2

Disharmony

Culture

In Paul de Man's criticism of Friedrich Schiller's aesthetic education, he accuses him of effectively teaching the metaphor of an organic society and in doing so being unable to teach philosophy. de Man's summary of the consequences of thinking education towards an organic society paves the way towards thinking a broader conception of educational experience which does not suffer the same limitations. For de Man, 'Schiller's considerations on education lead to a concept of art as the metaphor, as the popularization of philosophy.'[1] This means that rather than belonging to individuals in their singular experience, it is imposed on them as particulars of a social whole, so that, 'the aesthetic belongs to the masses. It belongs, as we all know – and this is a correct description of the way in which we organize those things – it belongs to culture, and as such belongs to the state, to the aesthetic state, and it justifies the state.'[2] Education, as the previous chapter has shown, is the dominant means by which this culture is produced, perpetuated, and justified, a culture which necessarily justifies the state and also itself: its particular form of education. A similar description of the state's relationship to culture and education is provided by Maurice Blanchot, so as to frame his discussion on the art that 'ungratefully' exceeds it:

> Culture is substance and full substance; its space is a continuous, homogenous space without gap and without curvature. Indeed, it grows and continues indefinitely; this is its power of attraction. Culture progresses; thus it has some emptiness in the direction of the future, but if it is in motion, it is also immobile by order of this motion, because it is becoming horizontal. The ground upon which it raises itself and to which it refers is still culture; its beyond itself, the ideal of unification and identification with which it merges. It could not be otherwise. Culture is right to affirm it: it is the labor of truth, it is the generosity of a gift that is necessarily felicitous. And the work of art is but the sign of the ungrateful and unseemly error for as long as it escapes this circle (which is always expanding and closing itself).[3]

Blanchot goes on to quote the poet, René Char, who claims that 'The new art will be an atheistic art.' For Blanchot this does not just refer to literal atheism but is also a repudiation of 'the principle in which God is but a support, and to attempt to leave the circle where we remain and have always remained enclosed in *the fascination of unity*, under his protection and under the protection of humanism – in other words, to leave (by which improbable heresy?) the enchanted knowledge of culture.'[4] To exceed the logic of humanist culture and humanist education is to be guilty of ingratitude and unseemliness, as far as that culture is itself concerned. To be against or outside the humanist legacy of education is to commit heresy against the generosity of its educational gifts and its offer of harmonious unity, even in its diminished or impoverished forms.

While the desirability of such a challenge or exit is paramount for Blanchot and de Man, it is perhaps also helpful to be reminded of Theodor Adorno's concern that moving away from an all-consuming logic of harmony might cause what he refers to as an 'allergic reaction' which 'wants to eliminate harmonizations even in their negated form' and that end up forming 'the self-satisfied transition to a new positivity.'[5] It would be easy to conceive of various innovations in 'democratic' or 'radical' education, for example, as simply being another, alternative (although analogous and often derivative), system of values. Of course, Adorno was referring to aesthetic harmony rather than social harmony but given that aesthetic education from Plato and Schiller to Herbert Read and beyond has continuously conflated the two, this warning can and should also be read in a social context. Rejecting one hierarchical imposition of harmony must not simply lead to another form of hierarchically imposed positivistic totality. To replace one set of values with another is still to be in thrall to value: the value of particular values, abstractly defined and productive of social orders by means of education. A broader conception of educational experience would not propose a new set of universal values relevant to all particular individuals within a particular social order but rather emphasises a regard for singular experience, even if it happens to be unsociable.

Unsociability

Unsociability is one of the primary targets of humanistic education in service of social order.[6] However, even as unsociability is rejected, challenged, or transformed, it acts as a resource for the forward movement of social and educational programmes. Unsociability is the fuel that must be burned in the name of social and educational progress. Immanuel Kant's *Idea for a Universal History with a Cosmopolitan Intent* (1784) exemplifies a philosophical tendency to perceive unsociability as a necessary resource for social progress. Culture redeems undesirable experience through the perpetuation of its own progress and development. The Fifth Thesis of this text is that, '[t]he greatest problem for the human species, whose solution nature compels it to seek, is to achieve a universal civil society administered in accord with the right.'[7] Art and culture, especially as transmitted through education, play a large part in achieving this because, '[a]ll the culture and art that adorn mankind, as well as the most beautiful social order, are fruits of unsociableness that is forced to discipline itself and thus through an imposed art to develop nature's seed completely.'[8] This relationship becomes especially pronounced when thought in terms of social progress and that which Kant sees as crucial to its perpetuation: war. However, it is not simply on the grounds of social order that Kant advocates the importance of war but also in terms of individual freedom. According to Kant, even though war and preparing for war are the greatest evil, they are also necessary both in terms of social liberty and progress.[9] It is precisely the evil of focusing on war that inspires progress, seemingly non-dialectically, because it can never be overcome or replaced if progress is to remain possible. The attention given to war and the attention given to progress are suspended in relation to one another; totally incompatible and yet complicit. Unlike the dialectical moment of the unsocial sociability *internal* to society, the impasse a society meets with *external* existential threat leads to internal harmony due in significant part to the external disharmony of perpetual war. By contrast, John Dewey takes a more obviously dialectical approach to social progress to redeem war and, implicitly, educational colonisation of what he calls 'savage tribes,'[10] as a means to educational progress:

> It is a commonplace that an alert and expanding mental life depends upon an enlarging range of contact with the physical environment. But the principle applies even more significantly to the field where we are apt to ignore it – the sphere of social contacts. Every expansive era in the history of mankind has coincided with the operation of factors which have tended to eliminate distance between peoples and classes previously hemmed off from one another. Even the alleged benefits of war, so far as more than alleged, spring from the fact that conflict of peoples at least enforces intercourse between them and thus accidentally enables them to learn from one another, and thereby to expand their horizons.[11]

While Kant is more concerned with war and education as a prerequisite means to social order and progress, Dewey sees social progress, notably through war and what seems to be at least allied with colonial expansionism, as a means to education. For Kant, social progress and order are as much the product of a shared social fear as individual and plural experiences and efforts. For him, culture is the product of social progress, which only occurs in states subjected to external danger. If there is no threat, either from war or unsociability, then there is no progress and no culture. For Kant, a progressive social order is possible because of education and war, whereas for Dewey, war and colonial expansionism are redeemable activities because they produce unparalleled opportunities for learning that ultimately contribute to a progressive social order. In a striking passage preceding his educational redemption of war and colonial expansionism, Dewey justifies these means through the educational reconstruction they might offer to the 'static and selfish' ideals of 'savage tribes' and assumes that reticence to colonial expansionism is primarily due to 'rigid adherence to their past customs':

> The essential point is that isolation makes for rigidity and formal insti-tutionalizing of life, for static and selfish ideals within the group. That savage tribes regard aliens and enemies as synonymous is not accidental. It springs from the fact that they have identified their experience with rigid adherence to their past customs. On such a basis it is wholly logical to fear intercourse with others, for such contact might dissolve custom. It would certainly occasion reconstruction.[12]

While Dewey's point is being made in the context of an argument on the alleged benefits of human association, its elisions and emphases, like Herbert Read's, are instructive. While he does not advocate explicitly for an edu-cation into a clearly defined culture or social order, he nonetheless has a particular vision of and reverence for his own version of humanist education as *the* means of social progress that is *necessarily* desirable, that supersedes its historically prominent oppressive and derogatory means and social and cul-tural effects. His focus on 'democratic' educational progress above all else permits him to state that, 'It remains for the most part to secure the intel-lectual and emotional significance of this physical annihilation of space.'[13] Here, then, is the socially outward-facing version of Kant's inward-facing disciplining of unsociability. For both Kant and Dewey, education and cul-ture are the product and means of the overcoming of unsociability in service of social and educational progress.

It is notable that these approaches to education rely on that which exceeds their values and coherence. They can only reject (or declare war on) that which remains asocial, sufficiently culturally different, and outside the dia-lectical limit of social progress thought through the relation between edu-cational society and its unsociable citizens or colonised peoples. Despite its educational efforts, the unsociality of the singular exceeds the social rather than providing a resource for its progress. Unsociability is a condition of existence, not a dialectical resource leading to social harmony. Statist prac-tices of aesthetic education tend to teach the expedient illusion of a harmony of educated individuals that promises a move away from unsociability towards shared values directed towards social progress. However, unsociability, and that which exceeds the social and its values, will never cease to exist and can even be utilised to undermine the narratives which proclaim the imposition of education as the means to social progress and order.

Søren Kierkegaard's description of the Tragic Hero from *Fear and Trembling* can be aligned with Kant's argument that social progress is only possible in the context of a threat of war. To give oneself up for the greater good, or to exist and act in the light of the possibility of that happening, generates a certain perspective on the individual's *particular* relation to the social. The severance from the social and ethical that the *singular* leap of Kierkegaard's Knight of Faith elicits is an example of what Kant describes as 'a fall to unredeemable corruption.'[14] By stepping outside or beyond prescribed social hierarchies and ethical norms, the Knight of Faith also steps beyond systems of value. Meaning becomes entirely singular and therefore redundant in terms of Kant's agenda of shared social progress, which is why, '[t]he true knight of faith is a witness never a teacher.'[15] The Knight of Faith does not prescribe, he only acts. The Tragic Hero, on the other hand, sacrifices himself in terms of shared values which could easily include collective existential threat or service to an educational mission. Action, for Kant, Dewey, and the Tragic Hero, can only be afforded value if it is understood by and in the social sphere. There is no space for that which cannot be understood by the dominant social order as social progress or social good, while at the same time the threat of war is insisted upon as its presupposition. For Kant, and perhaps Dewey, the necessity of prescribing a preference is clear: better war and/or colonisation than unsociability and lack of social progress through education. These preferences are based on a more general preference for mutual understanding to which Kierkegaard's Knight of Faith does not conform: 'A human being can become a Tragic Hero by his own strength, but not the Knight of Faith. When a person sets out on the Tragic Hero's admittedly hard path there are many who could lend him advice; but he who walks the narrow path of faith no one can advise, no one understand.'[16] Meaning can either be understood by others (for the Tragic Hero) or not (for the Knight of Faith). Without an already existing social and ethical educational context for meaning which plays into its value system, meaning falls flat as far as social value is concerned. This is, of course, not necessarily to speak against acting for others but rather emphasises the singularity of such acts, rather than only their fulfilment of an individual's educationally determined part in a larger social logic.

It is unsociability – which Kant suggests that education should discipline us against so as to be able to create a beautiful social order, and that Dewey sees primarily as an educational opportunity, whatever its form – that Kierkegaard might be seen as wanting to preserve rather than negate or redeem in terms of the social whole. This form of unsociability would not be thought primarily in terms of what might be called anti-social behaviour (although it could be, especially if perceived in terms of the social), the emphasis being rather on a de-prioritisation of imposed social logic than a direct attack on it. Kant seals off society from *singular* unsociable passions with the help of educational discipline, allowing instead for a form of passion to be generated by *particulars* as collective meaning in the face of the threat of annihilation. The singular is lost to the particular of the collective and the collective and its progression is shaped by potentially fatal engagement with other collectives. The Tragic Hero therefore finds himself sacrificed as a particular individual to Kant's sociability or Dewey's educational mission, while the Knight of Faith takes the leap of singular, unsociable meaning, which nonetheless might be in the service of others.

Redemption

The leap of Kierkegaard's Knight of Faith is, despite its religious connotations, indicative of a non- or anti-redemptive form of action. It is an action which is not concerned with or productive of the socially validated postural develop-ment of epistemological and moral rectitude deployed by the humanist legacy in education. It legitimates itself rather than being legitimated by a social and educational order. An illustration of another form of such an action, this time as a more obviously educational experience, can be found at the beginning of André Gide's memoir, *If It Die*, where he describes himself as a child crawling under a 'biggish table' with a 'table-cloth' that 'reached nearly to the ground,' with 'the concierge's little boy, who sometimes came to play with [him]':

> 'What are you up to under there?' my nurse would call out.
> 'Nothing; we're playing.' And then we would make a great noise with our playthings, which we had taken with us for the sake of appearances. In reality, we amused ourselves otherwise, beside each other but not with each other; we had what I afterwards learnt are called 'bad habits.'
> Which of us two taught them first to the other? I have no idea. Surely a child may sometimes invent them for himself. Personally, I cannot say whether anyone instructed me in the knowledge of pleasure or in what manner I discovered it – I only know that as far back as my recollection goes, I cannot remember a time without it.[17]

The individual and mutual education of co-masturbation, where the boys learn pleasure without obvious instruction, without even any obvious desire for one another, signals a mode of educational experience which exceeds and frustrates the aims of education as described by humanists and those in keeping with their legacy. Masturbation is, in this sense, parallel to the edu-cational leap of the Knight of Faith. The state of indecency or supposed moral and epistemological ignorance – as if pleasure were not itself a form of truth – is ripe for redemption through correct education but is not itself redeemable, except in the negative as 'miseducation.'

In *The Culture of Redemption*, Leo Bersani explores how the theme of redemption shaped the intellectual framework for Modernist art and liter-ature, as well as outlining the problems of this association. In the final part of his prologue, Bersani claims that, 'The self is a practical convenience,

promoted to the status of an ethical ideal, it is a sanction for violence' manifested principally in 'continuously renewed efforts to disguise and to exercise
the tyranny of the self in the prestigious form of legitimate cultural authority.' Bersani instead suggests that, 'To trace some of the narcissistic retreats
and intensities of literature may at least help us to think of art, and teach us to
want an art, unavailable for any such legitimizing plots.'[18] This, as the pedagogical task of Bersani's text, also, alongside the indecent education figured
by the experience of Gide and the concierge's boy, set the terms within which
a broader conception of education can be developed.

In Bersani's words, 'The culture of redemption might be thought of as
the creation of what Nietzsche called the theoretical man − who Nietzsche
claimed first appeared in the West in the person of Socrates − the man who
attributes to thought the power to "correct" existence.'[19] For Nietzsche, the
theoretical man abstracts philosophy from life, while for Bersani the culture
of redemption reads art as if it was philosophy, in the sense that it also is attributed the power to 'correct' existence. The experientially validating logic that
Bersani argues is afforded to art in the culture of redemption is just as easily
applied to education, exemplified in the extreme by Dewey's argument for the
educative benefits of war and colonial expansionism. For Bersani:

> A crucial assumption in the culture of redemption is that a certain type
> of repetition of experience in art repairs inherently damaged or valueless
> experience. Experience may be overwhelming, practically impossible to
> absorb, but it is assumed − and this is especially evident in much ency-
> clopaedic fiction − that the work of art has the authority to master the
> presumed raw material of experience in a manner that uniquely gives
> value to, perhaps even redeems, that material.[20]

Education, as exemplified by Dewey, is often ascribed a similar function.
As Ansgar Allen writes in *The Cynical Educator*, that which Nietzsche called
'Socratism,' 'originated the belief that despite our ignorance everything
is knowable, and hence *teachable*.'[21] It is this educational logic, then, that
underpins − and is therefore not only analogous to − the culture of redemption that Bersani locates in art. Here a complex knot in the relationship
between education and redemption is encountered. How can the redemptive
logic of education be rejected when even Bersani wants to 'help us to think
of art, and teach us to want an art, unavailable for [the] legitimizing plots' of
the culture of redemption and the tyranny of the self? Is this in itself not a
redemptive educational task? And further, is Bersani not engaging in a form
of hyper-redemptive discourse by suggesting that even non-redemptive art
can serve an educational function? I would argue not, and that this is because,
in the same way that Bersani is able to distinguish between redemptive and
non-redemptive art, we might be able to distinguish between redemptive
and non-redemptive narratives of educational experience. Equally, to think

an education or to teach us to want an education which rejects the tyranny of the self, especially in terms of how our 'selves' are educationally imposed on us by authoritative others, is not to suggest that aesthetic experience is analogous to educational experience but rather that they can be the same experience. In this sense, *The Culture of Redemption* is an educational resource, not only because it teaches a mode of aesthetic relation that is irreducible to that imposed in state-regulated education systems, but also because that mode of relation is itself non-redemptively educational.

Redemptive and non-redemptive education are not two forms of education completely separated from one another, rather redemptive education is the lens through which broader educational experience is often perceived. It is grounded in the logic of Nietzsche's theoretical man, for whom education only occurs if abstract and repeatable knowledge is attained, as well as the logic of doing away with unsociability in the name of shaping souls disposed to social order and its progress. Redemptive education also exhibits the exercise and preservation of what Bersani, in the context of art, calls 'moral monumentality.'[22] In a footnote to the sentence preceding Bersani's use of this phrase, he makes reference to an essay by Herbert Marcuse, 'The Affirmative Character of Culture,' which 'defines the role of culture in a civilization anxious to divert human beings from their real material situation, and to suggest that the private realm of the soul, where high culture is enjoyed, somehow makes up for debased and unjust social conditions.'[23] While Marcuse, parsed by Bersani, argues that 'this cultural ideal … has best been exemplified by art,' I would suggest that this is only the case because of the distinctly pedagogical character of redemptive art, which is itself part of a broader redemptive educational programme and cultural disposition. In the culture of redemption, education and art exist to teach moral and epistemological monumentality and rectitude in accordance with the social order.

In *Gide's Bent*, Michael Lucey argues that received readings of Gide's *The Counterfeiters*, somewhat ironically, tend to take the title at face value and perceive the novel as opposing sincerity and inauthenticity.[24] Such readings are constituted by and constitutive of the pedagogical character of the culture of redemption. Lucey's reading, on the other hand, opens the possibility of understanding the novel as being concerned more broadly with the problematic relationship of experience to the redemptive demands of authenticity. As Lucey suggests:

> People haven't been talking about authenticity in *Les Faux-monnayeurs* [*The Counterfeiters*] for years without the discourse being there, in the mouths of the characters and in the mouth of the narrator as well. But if, as I have argued, the novel is punctuated by another discourse, if that sleepy discourse regularly disconcerts the characters, and if, rather than respecting the disconcerting effect, they run to notions such as Bernard's *suffisance*, to notions of self-possession and sincerity in order to

protect themselves, then the dominance of the categories of authenticity, self-sufficiency, sincerity should, as categories to which one phobically flees, become suspect – the flight to them could even be seen as symptomatic. Recourse to those categories, in other words, should not be taken as a matter of course. Bernard, for instance, flees, phobically from disconcertion into *suffisance*; he flees from a sense of himself as *epar, leger, nouveau* (scattered, alleviated, novel), from his life seen as punctuated by a series of discontinuous appendices.[25]

If for Lucey, then, the flight to 'authenticity, self-sufficiency, sincerity' is perceived as being symptomatic, my claim is that it is precisely symptomatic of the educational culture of redemption. As such, the superficial interpretations of the novel that Lucey rejects are themselves symptomatic of this culture. These readers, in Lucey's argument, are blinded to the non- or anti-redemptive character of the novel because of their own culturally symptomatic recourse to redemptive morality and epistemology. This is principally an educational problem. If it is not even possible to see non- or anti-redemptive experience as educational (except in the negative), then all experience is, as a matter of course, either reduced, returned to, or rejected by the logic of redemption so as to locate and (re)produce moral and epistemological rectitude, manifested in Lucey's reading of *The Counterfeiters* through the characteristics of 'authenticity, self-sufficiency, sincerity.'

While Lucey provides an astute, anti-redemptive reading of what he calls the 'sleepy discourse' of the novel, which, for him, is principally connected to sexuality, *The Counterfeiters* also contains many other anti-redemptive discourses. The discourse most relevant to the educational argument made in this book is that which utilises the demands of the culture of redemption to sustain a counterfeit non-relation to the unredeemable aspects of bourgeois life. This discourse of the unredeemable is shown by Gide to be the 'dark' underside of rectitude and authenticity; an underside which is recognised and utilised by the coin counterfeiters in the novel to be able to sustain their activities with a protective silence.

> 'The kids we want, you see, are those who come of good families, because then if rumours get about, their parents do all they can to stifle them.' (It is Cousin Strouvilhou who is talking in this way, while the two are having lunch together.) 'Only with this system of selling the coins one by one, they get put into circulation too slowly, I've got fifty-two boxes containing twenty coins each, to dispose of. They must be sold for twenty francs a box; but not to anyone, you understand. The best thing would be to form an association to which no one should be admitted who didn't furnish pledges. The kids must be made to compromise themselves, and hand over something or other which will give us a hold over their parents. Before letting them have the coins, they must

be made to understand that – oh! without frightening them. One must never frighten children. You told me Molinier's father was a magistrate? Good. And Adamanti's father?'

'A senator.'

'Better still. You're old enough now to grasp that there's no family without some skeleton or other in the cupboard, which the people concerned are terrified of having discovered. The kids must be set hunting; it'll give them something to do. Family life as a rule is so boring! And then it'll teach them to observe, to look about them. It's quite simple. Those who contribute nothing will get nothing. When certain parents understand that they are in our hands, they'll pay a high price for our silence. What the deuce! We have no intention of black-mailing them; we are honest folk. We merely want to have a hold on them. Their silence for ours. Let them keep silent and make other people keep silent, and then we'll keep silent too, Here's a health to them!'

Strouvilhou filled two glasses. They drank to each other.

'It's a good – it's even an indispensable thing,' he went on, 'to create ties of reciprocity between citizens; by so doing societies are solidly established. We all hold together, good Lord! We have a hold on the children, who have a hold on their parents, who have a hold on us. A perfect arrangement.[...]'[26]

This unredeemable discourse which makes a mockery of imposed and inherited social 'legitimacy' helps to reveal not only the hollowness inherent to the posture of rectitude, but also how it relies on actively silencing, displacing, or forgetting the unredeemable to sustain itself. Redemption's wilfully silent complicity with the unredeemable (mirroring the not-so-silent complicity Kant and Dewey declare, in different ways, between social progress and war) undermines its own conceits and reveals the pernicious reciprocity that is required to fuel them. In the same way that Bernard's phobic flight from 'scattered, alleviated, novel' experience to *suffisance* could be seen as symptomatic of the culture of redemption, the theoretical man, in Nietzsche's terms, experiences and often even requires that which he attacks or refuses to acknowledge. Fear of irredeemable life only provokes further abstraction and self-justification, rather than putting into question the circular logic of a culture sustained by a fear of its excess or failure; a culture seemingly less concerned with its tangible contributions to, for example, 'material situations' or alleviating 'debased and unjust social conditions.'

Notes

1 Paul De Man, *Aesthetic Ideology*, trans. Andrzej Warminski (Minneapolis, MN: University of Minneapolis Press, 1996), 154.
2 Ibid., 154.

3 Maurice Blanchot, 'The Great Reducers,' in *Friendship,* trans. Elizabeth Rottenberg (Stanford, CA: Stanford University Press, 1997), 71.
4 Ibid., 72.
5 Theodor Adorno, *Aesthetic Theory,* trans. R. Hullot-Kentor (Minneapolis, MN: University of Minneapolis Press, 1997), 159.
6 Small parts of this chapter, primarily from this section, were previously published in much less developed form as: Emile Bojesen, 'Negative Aesthetic Education,' in *Against Value in the Arts and Education,* eds. E. Bojesen, S. Ladkin, and R. McKay (London & New York: Rowman and Littlefield, 2016), 395–414.
7 Immanuel Kant, 'Idea for a Universal History with a Cosmopolitan Intent,' in *Perpetual Peace and Other Essays,* trans. T. Humphrey (Cambridge: Hackett, 1983), 33.
8 Ibid., 33.
9 Ibid., 57.
10 John Dewey, *Democracy and Education* (London: Macmillan, 1966), 86.
11 Ibid., 86.
12 Ibid., 86.
13 Ibid., 86.
14 Kant, 'Idea for a Universal History with a Cosmopolitan Intent,' 67.
15 Søren Kierkegaard, *Fear and Trembling,* trans. Alasdair Hannay (London: Penguin, 2005), 96.
16 Ibid., 78–79.
17 André Gide, *If It Die,* trans. Dorothy Bussy (Harmondsworth: Penguin, 1977), 9.
18 Leo Bersani, *The Culture of Redemption* (Cambridge, MA: Harvard University Press, 1990), 4.
19 Ibid., 2.
20 Ibid., 1.
21 Ansgar Allen, *The Cynical Educator* (Leicester: Mayfly, 2017), 172.
22 Bersani, *The Culture of Redemption,* 22.
23 Ibid., 212.
24 Michael Lucey, *Gide's Bent: Sexuality, Politics, Writing* (Oxford: Oxford University Press, 1995), 109.
25 Ibid., 142.
26 André Gide, *The Counterfeiters,* trans. Dorothy Bussy (Harmondsworth: Penguin, 1966), 237–238.

Chapter 3

Domestication

Thought and purpose

For Ivan Illich, the 'hidden curriculum,' which supplies 'the message that only through schooling can an individual prepare for adulthood in society'[1] pervades and manipulates individuals across almost every aspect of social life. But, for him, it is school itself that 'enslaves more profoundly and more systematically, since only school is credited with the principal function of forming critical judgment, and, paradoxically, tried to do so by making learning about oneself, about others, and about nature depend on a prepackaged process.'[2] Only liberation from school can escape this process, which, Illich attests, is a position that even 'self-styled revolutionaries' are reluctant to take because there are themselves 'victims of school' and 'see even "liberation" as the product of an institutional process.'[3]

Illich's argument resonates with that made by Ian Hunter, for whom, 'Marxian theory is no less concerned than liberalism with reconciling the disciplinary character of schooling with the exercise of free judgment, and with harmonising the bureaucratic character of educational administration with democratic decision making.'[4] Radical political ideas are, for both Hunter and Illich, often domesticated to and by schooling. While egregious for Illich, Hunter's perspective – which is much more accommodating to what he sees as the unavoidability of schooled society – is that the radical educator is a useful resource for the very system they critique:

> It is as a 'virtuoso of conscience' that the teacher exerts the ethical power that joins self-examination and surveillance, self-discovery and obedience, and holds together the basic ritual of our pedagogy. But this conscience is typically formed and displayed in that practice of secular holiness through which the pastoral intelligentsia withdraw from the worldly system of education that forms and employs them. This explains an otherwise paradoxical fact: that today the radical educator is, as the foremost virtuoso of conscience, the foremost exponent of pastoral discipline in the school system.[5]

It might, for example, seem as if Jacques Rancière's reading of Joseph Jacotot in *The Ignorant Schoolmaster* would provide the model of a teacher who escapes the humanist legacy and leaves room explicitly for broader educational experience, given that he emphasised the emancipatory qualities of education without explication and, in the most famous example of his teaching experience, could not speak the language of his students.[6] However, Jacotot is instead the instructor *par excellence*, relying on problems so ready-made and contextually delimited in and by the classroom that the 'solutions' are obvious to the students and they do not even require much elaboration from their instructor.

The ignorant schoolmaster knows precisely what is to be instructed and its value, even if he does not know the content of it himself. The master also continues to hold the student accountable: 'The ignorant master must demand from his student that he prove to him that he has studied attentively.'[7] It is therefore possible to suggest that (perhaps in ideological contrast to the positions Rancière takes up elsewhere) the ignorant schoolmaster might in fact be the ultimate 'neoliberal educator' or instructor: an accountant of attentiveness and effort, as well as a facilitator and attributor of value. He is not only able to instruct students in what is considered valuable to their culture without any prior knowledge of the subject – which means that the education of such an educator would be extremely time and cost effective – supposedly in the name of equality, he judges them not on their ability but on their attentiveness.

In *The Ignorant Schoolmaster*, almost the entire responsibility for educational success is transferred onto the effort of the student, without any apparent sensitivity to individual context or interest (including, of course, structural inequalities that might affect them despite their assumed equality). There may also be interesting but problematic correlatives between Rancière's logic of 'equal intelligences' and that of 'equality of opportunity,' in the sense that treating all students as if they had equal intelligence might have disastrous consequences for those who have very different kinds of intelligence (however equal) to their classmates. Either way, the development of the virtues of attention, effort, autonomy, and individual responsibility become the underpinning objects of instruction. The ignorant schoolmaster is not the facilitator of some more enlightened form of education but rather actively attends to the attention given to the work, so that the student can learn its meaning and so that it has value; so that the student can 'solve' the ready-made 'problem' that has been set. Nowhere does this educational logic exceed that of the broader humanist logic of education and the educated person, and the special place it confirms for this form of education in society. The student must still be subject to contagion by the humanistic logic of education as necessary activity. The teacher's duty is not only to instruct, it is also to infect the student with the logic and specific sense of their community.

In *How We Think*, John Dewey describes the difference between the instructor and the teacher as beginning at 'the point where communicated matter stimulates into fuller and more significant life that which has entered by the straight and narrow gate of sense perception and motor activity.'[8] For him, 'genuine communication involves contagion' and the production of a 'community of thought and purpose between child and the race of which he is the heir.'[9] In Dewey's reading, the distinctive duty of the teacher as opposed to the instructor is the ability to be able to subject the child to contagion, specifically that of the thought and purpose of the community, suggesting that education is only worthy of the name when it enhances the relation between individual and community, and only ever in a purposive manner. The contagion of the individual with shared social thought and purpose is simply another form of education as social instruction, even if part of that instruction is the development of one's individual capacity to demo-cratically contribute to and change a society. Reading Dewey's description into Rancière's, far from emancipating the students, they are rather subject to contagion by Rancière's Jacotot and the self-reliance and personal respon-sibility now key to conceptions of educational success; conceptions which focus on agency, activity, and productivity.

Unlike Dewey, Jacques Derrida was often directly critical of the notion of community, thereby putting one of Dewey's main ends and means for education into question. Dewey's biological metaphor of communal conta-gion can be read against Derrida's insistence on the auto-immunity implicit in individuals and communities, without which 'nothing would ever hap-pen or arrive.'[10] For Derrida, individuals and relationships exist because of their non-presence to themselves and one another, and auto-immunity is concerned with the maintenance of non-self-certainty and openness to the always unexpected arrival of the other; an other which is not necessarily or even commonly 'another person' but rather that which one cannot already conceive of or invent within a singular context. This is described by Derrida as a condition of experience rather than as a proclamation for 'right' education.

What might be called the auto-immune condition in education would emphasise that the subjects of Dewey's communal contagion necessarily remain open to thought and experience which exists outside of the thought and purpose of their perceived communities and selves. Because, in Derrida's reading, both the individual and their relationships are conditioned by auto-immunity: it deconstructs ourselves, and allows them to change, to be educated, to be affected. By the same dint, for Derrida, there is no commu-nity *per se*, only auto-co-immunity or the auto-immunity we all have in common. This is why social harmony cannot be a legitimate aim of educa-tion, as it is at once impossible, and its logic is ultimately anti-educational. To be immunised is to be closed off towards that which could change or put into question the self-present individual or community. In this sense, Dewey's contagion would also be a form of immunisation. Or to read it another way, Dewey's contagious education takes advantage of and perhaps abuses the con-dition of auto-immunity. In these terms, his model of education would be the contagion of the students with something which then shuts out unsociable or anti-social others – and, in fact, any distractions from the progression of the greater educational logic – by immunising against their influence. This is the logic of anti-education and the fossilisation of form.

The job of Dewey's teacher would be to immunise the student against that which exceeds what is considered useful for the progress of the individual and society, thus immunising them against anything that strays too far from the legacy of humanist education. From a Derridean perspective, this would not only be existentially impossible but also politically suspect. Dewey's Hegelian 'principle of the continuity of experience' implies, in his own words, that 'All ends and values that are cut off from the ongoing process become arrests, fixations. They strive to fixate what has been gained instead of using it to open the road and point the way to new and better experiences.'[11] A broader conception of education, on the other hand, would be just as stimulated by these arrests and fixations. Auto-immunity means that students' capacity for the formation of form remains open both in theory and practice. It also means that what they think or who they think they are can be destroyed by their very own thought. This 'very own' thought might come as if from elsewhere.

Fourier and anarchist education

Anarchism, historically, has legitimated various forms of 'integral education,' which emphasised bringing together practical and intellectual education, rather than separating them out from one another. The term and approach was coined by Charles Fourier,[12] was expounded in substance by Pierre-Joseph Proudhon,[13] and was agreed upon by the First International, notably with significant support from Mikhail Bakunin in articles on the subject for *L'Égalitié* as early as 1869.[14] Later, Peter Kropotkin presented a version of 'integral education' in his book, *Fields Factories and Workshops*, published in 1898.[15] Some of those who accepted the theoretical legitimation of this form of education, such as Paul Robin, Sébastien Faure, and, perhaps most notably, Francisco Ferrer, went on to practice and promote versions of it themselves well into the twentieth century. Unlike his anarchist inheritors, though, Fourier specifically conceived of education as *not* taking place within a school, Modern or otherwise.[16]

While anarchist educational models are most usually consciously non-authoritarian and permissive forms of education, they generally leave intact the logic of humanist education. They supply a 'better' education but do not themselves question the inherited necessity of formalising education in settings consciously abstracted from broader social life and educational experience. They rather deign to improve upon that formalisation, thus, ultimately, allowing it to be justified, redeemed, and even legitimated as the very means of a just and legitimate society. This is not to dismiss these relatively anti-authoritarian initiatives out of hand, not least because, in their contexts, and even in a contemporary context, they at least challenge the authority of the state and put into question its modes of educational practice. However, despite their anti-authoritarianism, they fall into the trap of leaving one authority undiminished: that of the humanist legacy of education, where the educated person is, by virtue of that education, freer than they would otherwise have been precisely (and, of course, paradoxically) through their subjection to a particular educational method. Herein lies the problematic logic of Bakunin's oft-cited claim that 'Children do not constitute anyone's property; they are not the property of their parents nor even of society. They belong only to their own future freedom.'[17] Much less frequently invoked, though, are the sentences which follow:

> But in children this freedom is not yet real. It is only potential; for real freedom, that is, the full awareness and the realization thereof in every individual, pre-eminently based upon the feeling of one's dignity and upon genuine respect for the freedom and dignity of others, that is, upon justice – such freedom can develop in children only by virtue of the rational development of their minds, character, and rational will.[18]

Indeed, this entire digression on education by Bakunin is framed on the basis of educational compulsion: 'The upkeep, upbringing, and educating of the children of both sexes until they become of age, it being understood that scientific and technical training, including the branches of higher teaching, is to be both equal for and compulsory for all.'[19]

Nothing could be further from Fourier's vision. For him, to legitimately become a free member of society one would not need to undergo any sort of compulsion, and would instead be guided initially and primarily by enjoyment and interest:

> The education received by each child in incoherent societies varies according to the whims of teachers or fathers and has nothing in common with the purposes of nature, according to which children should turn their hands to all sorts of work, changing from one to another almost hourly. In the combined order this is what they will do, and as a result they will acquire amazing strength and dexterity because they will be constantly active, always doing different things, and never doing any one thing for too long.[20]

Fourier was not without his own questionable beliefs in educational redemption, arguing that under a freer society, 'Mental faculties will be developed more rapidly: I estimate that about twelve years will be enough to change those *living automata* we call peasants, who are so coarse as to be closer to the animal than human species, into men.'[21] However, his criticism is not based on the assumption that an *imposed* social order and compulsory education would transform the peasants, but rather that existent social restrictions and exigencies halt them from being able to be free and therefore to learn freely. To this extent, the nineteenth- and early twentieth-century anarchists, such as Bakunin, Kropotkin, and Ferrer, develop domesticated alternatives of Fourier's more radical educational and social thought. This domestication may, in itself, have been conceived as necessary, so as to better be able to promote their ideas in a context where received understandings of education and its association with schooling were prominent. Better, perhaps, to fight for social and educational concessions that might be more easily conferred than propose changes that stray too far from 'legitimate' conceptions of educational experience and practice.

This logic necessarily falls back on to humanist assumptions about education, where, even if particular work, or attendance, is not compulsory, the social pressure or expectations of children to be educated in a formalised manner, at least partly abstracted from broader social life and experience, does not dissipate sufficiently. What this means, and what the history of state-legitimated education has shown, is that these ideas can be co-opted and re-purposed by the state, in the guise of, for example, child-centred education and free schools, still serving the same function as any other school that predisposes the child towards the state, the current social order, and, as always, its limited, humanist conception of education. These co-options strengthen the state precisely in making it seem gentler and less directly harsh in its discipline. This is the (unavoidable?) trap that many critics of education today also fall into: they often desire a kinder, gentler, more pluralistic education, rather than, for example, the abolition of schooling and all of the inegalitarian privileges and disadvantages it has brought about.

This, then, is the unintended outcome of redeeming the legacy of humanist education, even provisionally and in a manner that is nonetheless grounded in anarchist principles. In stepping back from contemporary education into more explicitly humanist discourse around education, even anarchist efforts for a 'more fully human' education that avoid imposed authority or direct compulsion still rely on the naturalised or naturalising discourse of education. Where, by claiming to make us more fully human, imposed education is itself legitimated as necessary, as if it were a natural process. This, again, ignores that social relations are themselves broadly educative and that individuals, including children, are able to determine which social relations they want to enter into and how they would like to occupy their time. By socially compartmentalising education as occurring only or mainly in the context of schooling, these facts are obscured, and by naturalising school (even the Modern School or in hybrid forms of integral education) as the only or primary means of education, the social compulsion for relating to education *as* schooling remains. Delimiting education in this manner is based on the desire to grow an already existing social logic, rather than allowing it to be transformed directly by the individuals who constitute it.

Individual and society

Having more in common with Fourier's rejection of the civilisational legacy of humanism, Max Stirner was entirely against the teaching of knowledge, preferring 'self-development.' In his view, 'pedagogy should not proceed any further towards civilizing, but toward the development of free men, sovereign characters; and therefore, the will which up to this time has been so strongly suppressed, may no longer be weakened.'[22] Nietzsche's Zarathustra makes a similar claim: 'Willing liberates because willing is creating: thus I teach. And you should learn *only* for creating!'[23] As Stirner puts it: 'the necessary decline of non-voluntary learning and rise of the self-assured will which perfects itself in the glorious sunlight of the free person may be expressed somewhat as follows: *knowledge* must die and rise again as *will* and create itself anew each day as a free *person*.'[24] While Stirner took this thinking even further in the direction of the individual in *The Ego and His Own: The Case of the Individual Against Authority*, James Guillaume – one of the lone anarchists to inherit more directly from Fourier and take a firmer stand against schooling and humanist conceptions of education – developed similar principles in the direction of the social.

Guillaume did not only imagine an individual freed from authoritarian education but an entire society liberated from its influence and strictures. He was clear that his vision could 'be effectively achieved only by means of a revolutionary movement.'[25] Before anything else, 'there is the slow transformation of ideas, of needs, of the motives for action germinating in the womb of society' which is followed by 'a brusque and decisive turning point — the revolution — which is the culmination of a long process of evolution, the sudden manifestation of a change long prepared for and therefore inevitable.'[26] He describes 'the kind of revolution most attractive to us and the ways it can be freed from past errors.'[27] While its positive goal would begin by the taking 'possession of all capital and the tools of production,' its character

> must at first be negative, destructive. Instead of modifying certain institutions of the past, or adapting them to a new order, it will do away with them altogether. Therefore, the government will be uprooted, along with the Church, the army, the courts, the schools, the banks, and all their subservient institutions.[28]

Guillaume too, challenges the 'false principle' that 'the child as the personal property of the parents,' arguing that children belong to no one but themselves, and that 'during the period when he is unable to protect himself and is thereby exposed to exploitation, it is society that must protect him and guarantee his free development. It is also society that must support him and supervise his education.'[29] Importantly this education would not be imposed and would be responsive to context, especially across different communities, 'here they would have life in common, there they would leave children in care of the mother, at least up to a certain age, etc.'[30] It would also 'not be entrusted solely to a specialized caste of teachers; all those who know a science, an art, or a craft can and should be called upon to teach.'[31]

Guillaume outlines two stages of education, the first, 'where the child of five or six is not yet old enough to study science, and where the emphasis is on the development of the physical faculties.'[32] This stage will only focus on 'observation, practical experience, conversations between children, or with persons charged with teaching.'[33] Taking a distinctly Fourierian turn, Guillaume outlines the self-organisation of children in his utopia:

> No longer will there be schools, arbitrarily governed by a pedagogue, where the children wait impatiently for the moment of their deliverance when they can enjoy a little freedom outside. In their gatherings the children will be entirely free. They will organize their own games, their talks, systematize their own work, arbitrate disputes, etc. They will then easily become accustomed to public life, to responsibility, to mutual trust and aid. The teacher whom they have themselves chosen to give them lessons will no longer be a detested tyrant but a friend to whom they will listen with pleasure.[34]

Although Guillaume's ideas were never explicitly enacted, a similar approach was promoted by Shulamith Firestone in the 1970s, where she concluded that 'the irrelevancy of the school system practically guarantees its breakdown in the near future.'[35] Her suggestion was that schools could be replaced by 'non-compulsory "learning centres," which would combine both the minimally necessary functions of our lower educational institutions, the teaching of rudimentary skills, with those of the higher, the expansion of knowledge, including everyone of any age or level, children and adults.'[36] In her view,

> the amount of rote knowledge necessary either for children or adults will itself be vastly reduced, for we shall have computer banks within easy reach. After all, why store facts in one's head when computer banks could supply quicker and broader information instantaneously? (Already today children wonder why they must learn multiplication tables rather than the operation of an adding machine.) Whatever mental storing of basic facts is still necessary can be quickly accomplished through new mechanical methods, teaching machines, records and tapes, and so on, which, when they become readily available, would allow the abolition of compulsory schooling for basic skills.[37]

While Firestone may be right that these technological innovations, which have now come to fruition, perhaps even beyond the expectations of her imagination, might allow for the abolition of compulsory schooling for even basic skills, the domesticating impulse of educational thought and practice sustains the status quo, underpinned by the redemptive logic of the humanist legacy, where any thought of liberation from imposed education is supplanted by a particular notion of liberation made possible by a particular form of compulsory education. In the same year that Firestone published *The Dialectic of Sex*, 1970, Pierre Klossowski published his *Living Currency*, where he argued that

> To overcome the punitive character of labour in communal life (which entailed not only the communal ownership of the means of production but also of individuals), the production of objects, even useful objects, would no longer be done in accordance with *an industrially determined need* but rather with a *passional aspiration*. Work would be performed in the euphoria of the imagination as the spontaneous and creative activity of humanity.[38]

This explicitly Fourierian utopian social thought coheres with Firestone's but is more reliant on a reconfiguration of individual and social dispositions than the opportunities of technological resources. In an essay, 'Sade and Fourier', published the same year, Klossowski argued that 'Fourier's prophecy of future (namely utopian or as yet non-existent) happiness contains an *explicit* critique of the existing economic system.'[39] His utopian projections 'enabled him to launch a scathing attack on the manners and grotesque conditions of the society of his time.'[40] Fourier also captured the interest of Italo Calvino, who, in 1971, described, with sympathy, several features of his thought relating to children and education:

> The most famous and extraordinary *trouvaille* of Fourier as an educator is that of the Little Hordes. Those children who like to play with muck — which is to say the vast majority — are organized into Little Hordes and are responsible for collecting the garbage. Thus what in Civilization is a vice becomes in Harmony a passion much appreciated by society, and what in Civilization is a repellent chore becomes in Harmony a game that answers to the inner vocation. Instead of being looked down upon, the Little Hordes are surrounded by the veneration of the public, their members are thought of as little saints, and this prestige stimulates their dedication to the common welfare.[41]

While hardly representative of the utopian society that Fourier envisaged, we do not have to look too far back in history or too far afield, geographically, to find examples of broader conceptions of pre- and non-humanist educational societies. Nicholas Orme explains that most people, in Medieval England, a mostly 'pre-school' society:

> learnt through work rather than at school. Even literary skills such as keeping accounts and writing them up, which could be acquired from

specialist teachers, must often have been mastered 'on the job' as an apprentice or a trainee clerk in a household. The process of learning to work starts early in life, for even young children take pleasure in copying adults and helping them with tasks [...] small girls followed their mothers in cooking or drawing water, while small boys were attracted to their fathers' work with tools and animals. Coroners' inquests and cases of trespass and damage show how older children gradually became involved in doing such tasks themselves. Already before they were seven, when they were still infants in medieval parlance, they might have been given simple household duties such as looking after younger siblings or fetching water from the well. Once they were seven or so, their liking to wander and explore could be utilised for the benefit of their families. Records show them gathering fruit and nuts, fishing in rivers, collecting shellfish on the shore, harvesting reeds in marshland, finding firewood, or digging peat from a turbary.[42]

It is also not the case, as Philippe Ariès famously suggested,[43] that there was no such thing as childhood in the Middle Ages, and that children weren't afforded an education simply because they were treated as adults, expected to work. To the contrary, Orme argues that historical evidence suggests 'that adults regarded childhood as a distinct phase or phases of life, that parents treated children like children as well as like adults, that they did so with care and sympathy, and that children had cultural activities and possessions of their own.'[44] Even though one might still be critical of the emphasis on education for labour, there may, nonetheless, be positive, rather than only condemnatory lessons to be learned from childhood and education in the Middle Ages. The point, though, is not to suggest that historical examples, or utopian propositions, such as those of Firestone, Guillaume, or Fourier, should be implemented, or the educational culture of the Middle Ages returned to, but rather to help to show how closed, calcified, limited, and limiting contemporary conceptions of education have become.

Notes

1 Ivan Illich, *Deschooling Society* (London: Marion Boyars, 1971), 70.
2 Ibid., 47.
3 Ibid., 47.
4 Ian Hunter, *Rethinking the School* (St Leonard's: Allen and Unwin, 1994), 22.
5 Ibid., 168.
6 Small parts of this section of this chapter were published in much less developed form as: Emile Bojesen, 'Passive Education,' *Educational Philosophy and Theory*, 50:10 (2018), 928–935.
7 Jacques Rancière, *The Ignorant Schoolmaster: Five Lessons in Intellectual Emancipation*, trans. Kristin Ross (Stanford, CA: Stanford University Press, 1991), 31.
8 John Dewey, *How We Think* (Boston, MA: D.C. Heath & Co, 1910), 224.
9 Ibid., 224.

10 Jacques Derrida, *Rogues: Two Essays on Reason*, trans. Pascale-Anne Brault and Michael Nass (Stanford, CA: Stanford University Press, 2004), 152.

11 John Dewey, *The Political Writings* (Cambridge: Hackett, 1992), 244.

12 Paul Avrich, *The Modern School Movement: Anarchism and Education in the United States* (Chico, CA: AK Press, 2006), 15–17.

13 Pierre-Joseph Proudhon, *Property is Theft!: A Pierre-Joseph Proudhon Anthology*, ed. Iain McKay (Chico, CA: AK Press, 2011), 378 and 593–594.

14 Robert Graham, *We Do Not Fear Anarchy We Invoke It: The First International and the Origins of the Anarchist Movement* (Chico, CA: AK Press, 2015), 78–79 and 162–163.

15 Peter Kropotkin, *Direct Struggle Against Capital: A Peter Kropotkin Anthology*, ed. Iain McKay (Chico, CA: AK Press, 2011), 643–645, and 669–671.

16 Charles Fourier, *The Theory of the Four Movements*, trans. Ian Patterson (Cambridge: Cambridge University Press, 1996), 14 and 68–69.

17 Mikhail Bakunin, *The Political Philosophy of Bakunin: Scientific Anarchism*, ed. G. P. Maximoff (London: The Free Press, 1953), 343.

18 Ibid., 343.

19 Ibid., 343.

20 Fourier, *The Theory of the Four Movements*, 68–69.

21 Ibid., 69.

22 Max Stirner, 'The False Principle of Our Education or, Humanism and Realism,' *The Anarchist Library*. https://theanarchistlibrary.org/library/max-stirner-the-false-principle-of-our-education (accessed July 11, 2019), unpaginated.

23 Friedrich Nietzsche, *Thus Spoke Zarathustra*, trans. Adrian Del Caro (Cambridge: Cambridge University Press, 2006), 165.

24 Max Stirner, 'The False Principle of Our Education or, Humanism and Realism,' unpaginated.

25 James Guillaume, 'On Building the New Social Order,' in *Bakunin on Anarchism*, ed. and trans. Sam Dolgoff (London: Black Rose Books, 2002), 357.

26 Ibid., 357.

27 Ibid., 357.

28 Ibid., 357–358.

29 Ibid., 372.

30 Ibid., 372.

31 Ibid., 373.

32 Ibid., 373.

33 Ibid., 373.

34 Ibid., 374.

35 Shulamith Firestone, *The Dialectic of Sex* (London: Verso, 2015), 211.

36 Ibid., 211.

37 Ibid., 211–212.

38 Pierre Klossowski, *Living Currency*, trans. Vernon W. Cisney, Nicolae Morar, and Daniel W. Smith (London: Bloomsbury, 2017), 52.

39 Pierre Klossowski, 'Sade and Fourier,' in *Living Currency*, trans. Paul Foss-Heimlich (London: Bloomsbury, 2017), 81.

40 Ibid., 81.

41 Italo Calvino, *The Literature Machine*, trans. Patrick Creagh (London: Vintage, 1997), 216.

42 Nicholas Orme, *Medieval Children* (New Haven, CT: Yale University Press, 2001), 307.

43 Philippe Ariès, *Centuries of Childhood*, trans. Robert Baldick (London: Pimlico, 1996).

44 Orme, *Medieval Children*, 5.

Chapter 4

Expenditure

Ends

Education: ending and unending, vicious and violent in its circularity and repetition, rending and rendering. At once more banal and more profound than commonly conceived, in life it often has neither end nor ends. Education's only end is death. 'Ends' ascribed to education operate within the regime of what could be called anti-education; a purposeful limitation and proscription of an 'educational' milieu, functioning at the level of the operability of 'content' that purposefully closes down reflection on the experience of education, evacuating and distorting (in the name of clarity and orientation) experience in favour of anti-educational norms. For Peter Gelderloos, 'the fundamental purpose of education is to civilize children, and a large part of this means filling their heads with the lies that are necessary to make them always view history and society from the perspective that privileges state power.'[1] School is also the locus of 'the first heavily supervised play,' where, in the words of Shulamith Firestone:

> Children's natural enjoyment of play is now co-opted to better socialize (repress) them. ('Larry did the best fingerpainting. What a good boy! Your mother will be so proud of you!') In some liberal schools all the way up, it is true, good teachers try to find subjects and activities that will truly interest children. (It's easier to keep order that way.) But as we have seen, the repressive structure of the segregated classroom itself guarantees that any natural interest in learning will finally serve the essentially disciplinary interests of the school.[2]

A relentless violence is perpetrated against the breadth of educational experience in the very name of education. The educational violence of society, usually first manifested in the context of the family, imprisons the subject-to-be-educated for the ends of control. A socially legitimated and enforced education is considered necessary for individual survival only in a society that makes a particular form of imposed education a prerequisite of survival. As Ivan Illich puts it, 'Rich and poor alike depend on schools and hospitals which guide their lives, form their world view, and define for them what is legitimate and what is not.'[3]

Compulsory and obligatory education is most commonly practiced as a means of biopolitical intervention and control, designed to stabilise or even 'immunise' subjects, in order to prevent unintended forms of education taking place in the present and future. The basic function of so-called education systems, however progressive or conservative they might superficially seem to be, is the formation of subjects disinclined from educational experience in contradiction to or contradistinction from the most prescriptive (which is to say, already protentively inbuilt and prepared for) education:

> The contemporary ideal is a pan-hygienic world: a world in which all contacts between men, and between men and their world, are the result of foresight and manipulation. School has become a planned process which tools man for a planned world, the principal tool to trap man in man's trap.[4]

A public education system can be conceived of as a means to social 'hygiene,' as well as a self-preservative (both individual and more broadly social) means to economic productivity, which ultimately also comes under the hygiene function, in service of the contextually specific conceptions of 'health' (both physical and psychological) of the individual and socio-economic body. Pierre Klossowski might read this feature of contemporary social life as an example of what he describes as a repressive *external perversion that creates the conditions in which the unity of the individual can be affirmed.*[5] To escape it, and the false needs and ends it creates in individuals, often through various forms of explicit or implicit education, one must allow the individual unity one has been educated into to dissolve:

> The day human beings overcome, and thus subdue, this *external* perversion (the monstrous hypertrophy of their 'needs') and instead consent to their *internal* perversion (the dissolution of their fictive unity), a pact will be formed between desire, on the one hand, and the production of its objects in a rationally organized economy, in accordance with its impulses, on the other. Thus, the *gratuity of effort* will become the *price of the irrational*.[6]

While Klossowski's Fourier-inspired alternative implies the radical ethical transformation of human life, it also gestures towards a form of educational experience unfettered by the humanist legacy, alongside offering incisive means to critique contemporary conceptions and practices of education as 'external perversion' in the aid of a 'fictive unity,' perhaps of the state as well as the individual.

For a 'healthy' state or 'educated' individual, all expenditure is 'productive' if it is in the name of progressing that health or education. Jacques Derrida's notion of auto-immunity, discussed in the previous chapter, helps to deconstruct the perniciousness of the myth-like ideal of the healthy state, defined by its predominantly productive expenditure. Such a myth, hand in hand with the 'fictive unity' of the individual that Klossowski describes, artificially shuts down the conceptual possibility of productive expenditure counter to a state's interests, for example, in educational experiences and subject formations which are not considered healthy or productive. However, its educational structures are themselves an example of an unacknowledged 'unproductive expenditure,' to use a term from Georges Bataille; an expenditure which, in my own example, is 'productive' only within the absurd logic of a state's educational economy:

> Human activity is not entirely reducible to processes of production and conservation, and consumption must be divided into two distinct parts. The first, reducible part is represented by the use of the minimum necessary for the conservation of life and the continuation of individuals' productive activity in a given society; it is therefore a question simply of the fundamental condition of productive activity. The second part is represented by so-called unproductive expenditures: luxury, mourning, war, cults, the construction of sumptuary monuments, games, spectacles, arts, perverse sexual activity (i.e., deflected from genital finality) – all these represent activities which, at least in primitive circumstances, have no end beyond themselves.[7]

In a culture contaminated by the myth of social hygiene, manifested as what Klossowski calls a 'monstrous hypertrophy' of 'needs,' unproductive expenditure of energy, time, experience, and resource is castigated, except in as much as it can assist or replenish the capacity to serve those needs, thereby being redeemed as productive. This precipitates a 'process of degradation,' which, for Illich, 'is accelerated when nonmaterial needs are transformed into demands for commodities; when health, education, personal mobility, welfare, or psychological healing are defined as the result of services or "treatments."'[8] Education-saturated culture not only contributes to this hypertrophy of needs, but is also the most widespread and thoroughgoing example of how unproductive expenditure can be redeemed in the name of those needs. This process of redemption is the immune function at work in service of the myth of social hygiene.

Most educational practice aligned with the dominant logic of education can be understood as unproductive expenditure. Despite this, the hypertrophy of educational needs, requirements, and expectations continue, as do their cost to both states and individuals. The extent of the educational capture of populations, and their associated tax and debt burden, only grows. A distinctive feature of our absurdly inefficient educational economy is that it relies on being perceived as *productive expenditure*. This reliance is held up by the hypertrophy of needs, inherited from the humanist legacy of education, reproduced and continuously transformed and adapted by the educational economy, its advocates, and contributors. Even if this restrictive educational economy, to adapt a term of Bataille's, does not rely on a straightforward logic of scarcity, the humanist legacy locates a never fulfillable demand in the very subject to be educated. It is within this restrictive economy that

> Man's disregard for the material basis of his life still causes him to err in a serious way. Humanity exploits given material resources, but by restricting them as it does to a resolution of the immediate difficulties it encounters (a resolution which it has hastily had to define as an ideal), it assigns to the forces it employs an end which they cannot have. Beyond our immediate ends, man's activity in fact pursues the useless and infinite fulfilment of the universe.[9]

The ends of the concomitantly restrictive form of education inherited from humanism, then, are not materially determined ends, but rather humanistic ends, superimposed onto a restrictive educational economy. These 'needs' are not benignly, or even simply arrogantly, in service of the 'improvement' of the educational subject, rather they are crucial components in the hierarchical stratifications of societies. Equally, they continue to play a greater part in the growth of debt-based economies, with the educational lack at the core of every individual providing an infinite demand, the needs of which only a growing educational economy can hope to even partially or superficially fulfil. Ever-greater expenditure in the name of a demand constructed by the humanist legacy. Unproductive educational expenditure brought about by the hypertrophy of educational needs.

On the one hand, this lack of productive expenditure in the name of spurious educational needs – especially when requiring so much resource of various kinds, and the vast accumulation of personal and national debt – is clearly not redeemable by any measure. However, on the other hand, its irredeemability is itself an opportunity for reflection on the practice of unproductive expenditure more generally. In an important sense, the absurdity of the ever-expanding contemporary educational economy can be perceived as unintentionally prefiguring something nearing a post-work economy. If the recognition of its unproductive expenditure were coupled with its unlatching from the hypertrophy of needs that insures and drives it, the educational economy's bubble could be punctured in a manner that did not simply attempt to redirect its resources towards more productive expenditure. Indeed, the very notion of unproductive expenditure, coupled with a broadened conception of education beyond the humanist legacy, registers an interest in a social economy more seriously concerned with entertaining socially irredeemable or valueless experience as a necessary but also *desirable* component of its constitution.

The inculcation of needs through education, as well as the perpetuation of the social need *for* a specific form and practice of 'productive' education, is at once illegitimate and unnecessary; its only obvious benefit as an enforced, compulsory, and quasi-compulsory system being to those who gain from the social and economic stratifications it produces and the creditors of the debt accumulated in its name. The 'need' for education based on the lack located in the subject-to-be-educated perceives the result of its process as a form of individual 'growth,' which is perhaps in many instances parallel to, but not the same as, the growth of the economy itself. However, this individualised 'growth,' as Bataille puts it, is instead, '[s]ubordinated existence postponed until later.'[10] Individual expenditure and consumption are opposed, in his understanding, to growth:

> There is not only joy or suffering: there is living in the present moment and living for the future, in other words, consumption or growth. In the case of growth, there is the being that does not exist yet, subordinated to the being that will be. I grow, therefore I do not exist yet, I expend, therefore I am. Thus the being is insofar as it is against the will to growth.[11]

As well as obligating the necessity of individual growth, the educational economy, and the various forms of education within it that are in inherited from the humanist legacy are dominated by the 'will to growth.' This will to growth is located in the subject-to-be-educated, as well as constitutive of the legitimating process of the entire educational economy. The growth produced by education is intended to be personal, social, and economic, in financial terms. Thus, the experience necessitated by subjection to the educational economy is framed by a logic antithetical to the satisfaction of individual expenditure as consumption. The individual does not consume this form of education, it consumes them; delaying their capacity for consumption to the point at which they are sufficiently educated, certified, qualified, and employed. Though, even then, the structural postponement of an education always-to-be-bettered can provide no consumptive satisfaction in and of itself, except in as much as it is undermined or exceeded.

Despite it now being common to describe education as a product and the student as a consumer, humanist education only gestures towards future consumptions that it makes possible, or at least intimates that it might. As such, on the one hand, the restrictive educational economy can be described as a vast project of unproductive expenditure, justified by 'superficial interpretations, granting an alleged purpose to something that essentially has no purpose.'[12] While, at the same time, it is also, on the other hand, the very means by which unproductive expenditures, unsullied by the hypertrophy of 'needs,' are deferred. In this sense, education is a corrupt and corrupting form of unproductive expenditure, devoid of the satisfactions Bataille attributes to the unproductive expenditure that should be associated with consumption. This is because the educational economy presents its version of education as utilitarian expenditure and growth, which, at best, would be justified by the delayed satisfaction of unproductive expenditure and consumption. Its illusory utility, though, is imposed by social force and precedent that fuels and draws from the educational economy, rather than being determined by the actual utility of the task undertaken and the knowledge learned. The conception of educational space at home in the educational economy legitimates the fact of its own utility.

Vicious Circles

The two short stories, or récits, in Maurice Blanchot's *Vicious Circles* illustrate two extremely restrictive economies of educational context and practice. *The Idyll* charts the experiences of a stranger dealing with a highly regulated and oppressive society that nonetheless posits itself as benign. The stranger refuses to take on and embody the education his hosts impose, and suffers the consequences. *The Last Word* describes a world where regulation and law has been abolished, and yet power and authority still maintain their restricting force, notably at the level of education, especially in deference to the supposedly better educated. Shortly before its apocalyptic conclusion, which no educated certainty is able to counter, the unnamed protagonist deconstructs his teaching relation to a classroom of children. Both of these stories present sociopolitical contexts where regulation and/or authority act to repress and malign the subjugated epistemologies of non-authoritative individuals. While *The Idyll* is more straightforward in its representation of an oppressive and highly regulated pedagogic culture, *The Last Word* attends to the consequences of the collapse of regulation without the concomitant collapse of assertions of authority. Freedom from regulation does not mean freedom from oppression and authority, and can even enable their growth and exaggeration.

The Idyll

In Blanchot's *The Idyll*,' the vagabond protagonist, who comes to be called Alexander Akim (although it is unclear if this is his name or a name he is assigned), is always perceived first, foremost, and until his death, as a stranger. This fact is crucial to evaluating the social and educational relations he experiences. Because his subject position is fixed, the way that other characters relate to him is almost always predetermined by norms they have themselves learned. His ultimate rejection of their lessons results in his death by torture. Long before this fate becomes apparent, Akim seems constantly wary of those he encounters. This is understandable, as the story contains multiple accusations of characters spying on one another and acting as stool pigeons ('These accusations of spying were frequent, and perhaps they were justified. After all, why not betray men you did not like?').[13] The lessons of the story's culture must be both learned and consistently enacted by its characters to be able to avoid punishment. Some of the key lessons and practices of this culture are in the name of order and effort. Notably, the unproductive expenditure that Akim and the other vagabonds are tasked with is noted as being difficult, boring, pointless, but necessary:

> The work consisted of taking the stones that were dug out of the mountain each day by the city laborers and carting them to a huge pit. In the heat of the sun this was an exhausting task, exhausting and useless. Why throw the stones in to this pit when special trucks would be coming afterwards to haul them away? Couldn't these trucks have been loaded right after the stones were dug up, when they were sitting there in neat piles? But the vagabonds had to be given work and vagabond work was never to any great purpose.[14]

Being forced to engage in this work contributes to Akim's development of a fever and, because he lets the director of the vagabonds know he feels he has been treated brutally, he is locked away in a dire cell where he is nonetheless cared for by an orderly. In an attempt to comfort Akim, the orderly attempts to educate him dialogically:

> 'Naturally,' he said, 'it's hard to have your freedom taken away from you. But is anyone ever free? Can we do what we want? And there are so many other reasons for being unhappy.'
> 'Thank you,' said Akim, 'but you won't console me with the thoughts of others' unhappiness. My suffering belongs to me.'[15]

After he is let out of this literal prison, an old man who is part of his work group lets him know he remains in a more diffused but still effective metaphorical prison: 'Everyone here has his own prison, but in that prison each person is free.'[16]

These lessons are compounded further in a bookshop where Akim is recommended a book on the Home:

> The work was illustrated with photographs and, as he expected, it was filled with praise for the penal methods that were such a source of pride to the State: the mixture of severity and gentleness, the combination of freedom and restraint – these were the fruit of long experience, and it was difficult to imagine a more just or reasonable system.[17]

The self-convinced utopianism of this just and rational system, with the meaningless work of unproductive expenditure at its core, is reminiscent of nationally regulated education systems (including those that are partly priva-tised), convinced that they are (or are very close to being) the most just and rational compromise between equality of opportunity and access, as well as limitations of resources. What if the Home was the school, the director its prin-cipal or headmaster, the moving of the stones the studying of soon-forgotten material for exams, each child free in their own prison and responsible for their conformity, as well as the consequences of non-conformity they may suffer?

After Akim has been both locked up and then released for voicing his suf-fering, the director's wife, Louise, asks him how she can help, and he responds simply, 'I am suffering because I am not free. Let me become the man I was before.'[18] But this is impossible, as becomes apparent when the director explains to Akim that 'you're in a house where we have your best interests in mind; you should leave it to us and not worry about unpleasant things.'[19] Teacher knows best.

On asking when he might be able to leave this Home, the director replies, seemingly in jest, that 'When you no longer feel like a stranger, then there will be no problem in becoming a stranger again.'[20] Finally, Akim, slowly becomes an ironic teacher of the lessons of the Home, telling a group of his fellow workers and prisoners that

> You'll learn that in this house it's hard to be a stranger. You'll also learn that it's not easy to stop being one. If you miss your country, every day you'll find more reasons to miss it. But if you manage to forget it and begin to love your new place, you'll be sent home, and then, uprooted once more, you'll begin a new exile.[21]

These words are reported to the director, presumably by a spy or stool pigeon, and result in a threat of punishment to Akim. After this Akim uses a false proposal of marriage to escape from the Home; as the law is that you may leave if you are married (presumably because you are sufficiently integrated into and committed to the society). Instead he elopes and attempts to escape the city but falls foul of a fever which allows him to be captured and returned to the Home, now carrying the burden of the additional crime of deceiving a young woman with a false proposal.[22] The result is that he is tortured so brutally that he dies, and the Home continues with its work under a 'superb and victorious sky.'[23] Difference, strangeness, and refusal of an education are all incompatible within the restricting economy of this culture. Each person learning to be 'free' in their own individual cell, distrustful of one another, and paranoid of the consequences of acting out. Here, dialogue can only result in conformity, consensus the result of the annihilation of anything but internalised and imprisoned difference.

Sarah Kofman's *Smothered Words* reads *The Idyll* in the context of a med-itation on how the figure of the Stranger is sustained within an 'idyllic' community, arguing that 'The law of the story and its economy is to bury all strangeness with the Stranger, to disguise the fact that the return of the Stranger in the night like a ghost passing through all the cracks in the house, far from bringing about its destruction and collapse, can alone provide a true foundation for the idyll.'[24] In this way, the stranger becomes the unsociable resource for the idyll's educational programme. The stranger performs the different roles of an enemy to war with, for Kant, and 'savage tribes' to educate, for Dewey, as discussed in this book's second chapter. At once an enemy and a subject to be redeemed, the stranger justifies and mobilises the resources of the community, regardless of his own perception of their illegitimacy. He must submit to the restricting, hygienic myths of their community by means of the superficially unproductive expenditure of moving the rocks, which is nonetheless productive as it is intended to educate him into his necessary submission to their hypertrophic needs.

The Last Word

Similarly to *The Idyll*, the world of *The Last Word* is historically highly regulated, with an hour of solitude and a daily watchword. However, as the story is intended to chronicle the collapse of this regulation, contrary to the first story, the subject positions of the characters seem much less fixed. A key example is that the teacher isn't defined or named as a teacher until he teaches, and identities seem to shift with their contexts and sometimes not be determinable at all (which is reminiscent of Blanchot's novel *The Most High*). It would seem to show that when you are a teacher, you are not a person, you are part of a socially insured and legitimated relation, which runs the risk of totalisation, hence the desire to unbind from and undermine, or at least add cautions to the role of the teacher. Even if the teacher states that they are not an authority, they do so with the authority of the teacher.

When it becomes apparent that the watchword has been abolished and that reading all books, rather than just those from the library, is permitted, the protagonist becomes upset and aggravated.[25] He runs to a pavilion where all of the children are being kept, and where the educational order has not yet been disputed, telling the reader that

> When I entered everyone became silent. Each child went to his place quietly, and, as the veil fell over the statue of the teacher, their heads lined up hypocritically on their desks. I stood in front of the small table beside the plaster statue and indicated that it was time for work to begin. Right away, they asked me the traditional question that is asked in schools: 'Are you the teacher or God?' I looked at them sadly. There were so many ways to answer them, but first I had to bring order to the class.[26]

He asks them to listen and tells them that he must speak with 'cries' and 'tears' and proclaims, 'Let's be friends.'[27] In the light of the doing away with the watchword he tells the students that now 'reading is free. If you think I talk without knowing what I'm saying, you are within your rights. I'm only one voice among many.'[28] After writing several passages on the blackboard he asks the students to 'cross out all these words and replace them with the word *not*.'[29] The children shower the protagonist, who has now become the teacher (in the narrator's phrasing), with affection and adulation, until 'a person the children themselves look upon with dread' appears, salivating and mute, although handsome.[30] The children turn against this new figure, hissing 'like vipers' until the teacher draws a picture of the 'young mute' on the blackboard, 'emerging from the mouth of a volcano amidst a shower of stones, rays of light, and garbage of every kind,' a figure the teacher calls 'our judge.'[31] He cries out, seemingly to the mute and the children, 'In the name of what will you judge us? Who will challenge you? Poor children. A wound like this is caused by language, and it imposes no restraints on you.'[32] The uproar on the part of the children grows and their mother screams for the teacher to give them back to her. Before leaving, he makes a final somewhat cryptic statement: 'The pupil listens to the teacher with docility. He learns his lessons from him and loves him. He makes progress. But if one day he sees this teacher as God, then he ridicules him and no longer knows anything.'[33]

From the classroom he runs to a tower (the last tower still standing), joined by a female companion whose body – perhaps with a reference to forms of embodied knowledge – has 'marks of fire' that seem 'to be forming the first shapes of a vague language.'[34] When they reach the tower they are confronted with its owner who proclaims himself 'the All Powerful One.'[35] The owner and the protagonist attempt to rest in the night and are woken by the woman's prophetic scream. She claims that 'The woods are on fire and the earth is shaking,' which the owner declares 'a woman's illusion' and that 'everything is peaceful. The night beats in vain against the walls of the city.' She continues to announce their imminent demise, as the owner continues to assure them all that they are safe: 'I've ruled over the world' he scolded, 'it shouldn't be so hard for me to make you be quiet.'[36] And so the story closes with the owner asserting his self-assumed authority, 'and when the tower collapsed and threw them outside, all three of them fell without saying a word.'[37] The woman's last words before this being, 'can't you feel that we're not standing on anything?'[38]

The owner's authority stands on nothing but obedience to it, nonetheless bringing about all of their deaths and the end of their world. Despite the loss of the watchword and its concomitant laws and regulation, respect for authority is not sufficiently unlearned. The owner 'knows' the truth and berates the woman for asserting an alternative. She is not sufficiently educated and not a person who could possibly have knowledge of any value compared to his own. The restricting social economy of authority and power excludes her knowledge and invalidates her 'illegitimate' education. Even in the face of death, he is not open to unlearning his privilege, so he may learn from her. And so, education falls back on illegitimate authority, legitimating itself, ultimately, only through force and privilege.

Notes

1 Peter Gelderloos, *Worshipping Power: An Anarchist View of Early State Formation* (Chico, CA: AK Press, 2016), 106–107.
2 Shulamith Firestone, *The Dialectic of Sex* (London: Verso, 2015), 89.
3 Ivan Illich, *Deschooling Society* (London: Marion Boyars, 1971), 2.
4 Illich, *Deschooling Society*, 110.
5 Pierre Klossowski, *Living Currency*, trans. Vernon W. Cisney, Nicolae Morar, and Daniel W. Smith (London: Bloomsbury, 2017), 66.
6 Ibid., 66.
7 Georges Bataille, ed., 'The Notion of Expenditure,' in *Visions of Excess: Selected Writings, 1927–1939*, trans. Allan Stoekl (Minneapolis, MN: University of Minnesota Press, 1985), 118.
8 Illich, *Deschooling Society*, 1.
9 Georges Bataille, *The Accursed Share: Volume 1*, trans. Robert Hurley (New York: Zone Books, 1991), 21.
10 Georges Bataille, *The Unfinished System of Nonknowledge*, trans. Michelle Kendall and Stuart Kendall (Minneapolis, MN: University of Minnesota Press, 2001), 161.
11 Bataille, *Nonknowledge*, 161.
12 Bataille, *Nonknowledge*, 244.
13 Maurice Blanchot, *Vicious Circles: Two Fictions and 'After the Fact,'* trans. Paul Auster (Barrytown, NY: Station Hill Press, 1985), 20.
14 Ibid., 7–8.
15 Ibid., 10.
16 Ibid., 10.
17 Ibid., 15.
18 Ibid., 14.
19 Ibid., 18.
20 Ibid., 19.
21 Ibid., 26.
22 Ibid., 28–33.
23 Ibid., 36.
24 Sarah Kofman *Smothered Words*, trans. Madeleine Dobie (Evanston, IL: Northwestern University Press, 1998), 30.
25 Blanchot, *Vicious Circles*, 42–43.
26 Ibid., 45–46.
27 Ibid., 46.
28 Ibid., 46–47.
29 Ibid., 47.
30 Ibid., 48.
31 Ibid., 48.
32 Ibid., 48.
33 Ibid., 49
34 Ibid., 52.
35 Ibid., 54.
36 Ibid., 55.
37 Ibid., 55.
38 Ibid., 55.

Chapter 5

Legitimacy

Myths

As is made evident in the foregoing chapter's readings of Blanchot's récits, beyond the myth of hygiene there are other legitimating myths, culturally deployed in nuanced ways. They include, for Ivan Illich, the myth of institutionalised values ('the belief that process inevitably produces something of value and, therefore production necessarily produces demand'), the myth of measurement of values (the initiation of 'young people into a world where everything can be measured, including their imaginations, and, indeed, man himself'), the myth of packaging values (where young people are sold 'a bundle of planned meanings, a package of values, a commodity whose "balanced appear" makes it marketable to a sufficiently large number to justify the cost of production' and where 'consumer-pupils are taught to make their desires conform to marketable values'), the myth of self-perpetuating progress (where 'expenditures to motivate the students to stay on in school skyrocket as he climbs the pyramid'), and the myth of unending consumption (where 'participation in the open-ended ritual is made compulsory and compulsive everywhere').[1] His claim is that 'No society in history has been able to survive without ritual or myth, but ours is the first which has needed such a dull, protracted, destructive and expensive initiation into its myth.'[2]

The self-obscuration of the legitimating process involved in supporting these myths is described by Pierre Bourdieu and Jean-Claude Passeron, where the '[l]egitimation of the established order by the School presupposes social recognition of the legitimacy of the School' which rests 'on misrecognition of the delegation of authority which establishes that legitimacy,' meaning that 'the educational system objectively tends, by concealing the objective truth of its functioning, to produce ideological justification of the order it reproduces by its functioning.'[3] The elitist and culturally myopic conceptions of what it means to be an 'educated person' (which vary but ultimately conform to conservative and hierarchical models, frequently manifested even in those perceived to be socially radical, on the left or the right) are the means to a mythical (but perhaps equally or more powerful) form of hygiene, that obscures the more basic hygiene function of compulsory education, often taking it for granted. The 'educated person' (an idea to be understood in all its cultural rarity and concomitant varieties of perniciousness) is not necessarily more able to perform particular practical activities but is, instead, able to 'see the world for what it is,' and, for example, understand what kind of subjectivities and social organisation should be accepted or changed (and with what they should be replaced). The truth has been revealed to the educated person. The educated person, though, is an illegitimate construct, that disposes of the possibility of broader experiences of education (as much as possible) in favour of experience that can be redeemed in terms of (anti-)education and exhibits its redemptive capacity in the guise of subsequent education through confirmation bias. It is the fossilisation of educational formation. Ignoring, as Peter Gelderloos puts it, that

> Like everyone else, children are capable of educating themselves, and are motivated to do so in the proper setting. But public schools rarely offer that setting, nor do they educate the students on topics of immediate usefulness, like surviving childhood, expressing emotions healthily, developing their unique creative potentials, taking charge of their own health or caring for sick people, dealing with gender violence, domestic abuse, or alcoholism, standing up to bullies, communicating with parents, exploring their sexuality in a respectful way, finding a job and apartment or making do without money, or other skills young people need to live.[4]

While the definition of what constitutes education can be broadened even further than Gelderloos,' as he suggests, a significantly more limited conception and practice of education is already projected onto young people and proliferated in society more generally. Compulsory education and educational culture operate on the condition that this limited conception of education determines the possibilities of educational experience, including limiting any significant problematisation of this received notion of education.

This limited conception of education and its establishment in theory and practice has turned education into what Gilles Deleuze calls an 'order-word,' which sets up ready-made problems that academics, teachers, and students work to 'solve,' even though it is the very framing of possible solutions that are the real problem. Education may even be a definitive and foundational order-word that frames and legitimates many others. In an early section of his book, ostensibly on Henri Bergson, *Bergsonism*, Deleuze writes, using the classroom as an example, about the oppression facilitated by the (anti-)educational framing of false social problems and their hamstrung solutions:

> We are wrong to believe that the true and the false can only be brought to bear on solutions, that they only begin with solutions. This prejudice

is social (for society, and the language that transmits its order-words [*mots d'ordre*], 'set up' [*donnent*] ready-made problems, as if they were drawn out of 'the city's administrative filing cabinets,' and force us to 'solve' them, leaving us only a thin margin of freedom). Moreover, this prejudice goes back to childhood, to the classroom: It is the school teacher who 'poses' the problems; the pupil's task is to discover the solutions. In this way we are kept in a kind of slavery. True freedom lies in a power to decide, to constitute problems themselves. And this 'semi-divine' power entails the disappearance of false problems as much as the creative upsurge of true ones.[5]

In contrast to this set-up, educational experience, rather than only anti-educational experience, happens every day for everyone. But, problematically, as Gelderloos, Firestone, and Deleuze have helped to show, these broader educational experiences are not usually conceived as such and are often actively excluded or completely ignored, especially in terms of their educational attributes. What this means is that only educational experiences that can sustain or reinforce already revealed 'truths,' especially when they appear as 'solutions' to ready-made problems, are considered legitimate. Michel Foucault describes the educational situation in the school similarly:

> Whereas the examination with which an apprenticeship ended in the guild tradition validated an acquired aptitude – the 'master-work' authenticated a transmission of knowledge that had already been accomplished – the examination in the school was a constant exchanger of knowledge; it guaranteed the movement of knowledge from teacher to the pupil, but it extracted from the pupil a knowledge destined and reserved for the teacher.[6]

We do not see how education tears us asunder, only how it propels us forward on the route anti-education has already prepared and continues to reveal.

What is commonly invoked when conceptualising education is an assumption that the most socially important and useful aspects of it are experienced and produced in institutional contexts, typified by the school and the university. At the same time, the absence of 'real education' or at least a more substantial education is often bemoaned. But if the only places where a real education is possible are often places where real education does not occur then society is itself in a kind of debt to this possible education that does not occur.

Projecting backward

In *Bergsonism*, Gilles Deleuze describes the future 'real' as the producer of the present 'possible' rather than the other way around. In his reading, the real 'project[s] backward' and conditions what is considered possible.[7] We can see how this relationship plays out in contemporary educational contexts, where the projected outcome circumscribes what is possible and even desirable in and through educational experience: we know exactly what is intended to be produced (grades, civic disposition) and why (jobs, social harmony). In opposition to this relationship between the real and the possible, Deleuze also locates in Bergson the concepts of the virtual and the actual, which are associated with the production of difference and creativity. It is one thing to be excited about the pedagogical potential of these latter concepts but the less pleasant task is, perhaps, to negotiate our relationship to the seemingly intractable and magnetic integration of the real and the possible in contemporary educational institutions.

There are two distinct uses of the Deleuzo-Bergsonian 'real' that can be applied to the context I describe. The first, as discussed by Deleuze in *Difference and Repetition*, is that the 'virtual' is real in so much as it is experienced: 'The virtual is opposed not to the real but to the actual. *The virtual is fully real in so far as it is virtual*.'[8] The second is that there are elements of the relationship between the virtual and the real which are interrupted or structured by the 'possible.' The 'possible' is an object of concern for Deleuze as he feels it distorts the present 'real' by being projected back, as if from a future 'real.' As he writes in *Bergsonism*:

> The real is supposed to resemble [the possible]. That is to say, we give ourselves a real that is ready-made, preformed, pre-existent to itself, and that will pass into existence according to an order of successive limitations. Everything is already *completely given*: all of the real in the image in the pseudo-actuality of the possible. Then the sleight of hand becomes obvious: If the real is said to resemble the possible, is this not in fact because the real was expected to come about by its own means, to 'project backward' a fictitious image of it, and to claim that is was possible at any time, before it happened? In fact, it is not the real that resembles the possible, it is the possible that resembles the real, because it has been abstracted from the real once made, arbitrarily extracted from the real like a sterile double.[9]

It can do this in more or less pernicious ways, the worst and falsest of which would be the projection of the fact that education (its content or outcome) is inherently good or edificatory, and that particular, limited (and often hierarchically organised) versions of it should be compulsorily imposed on to young people in a supposedly legitimate manner. Less pernicious, but more concerning for those at war with instrumentality, is the projection of real educational experience being lost because of a focus on outcomes (grades, jobs, etc.).

Education, in a broader sense, is no doubt experienced in these institutions, even if it is considered suboptimal. Concomitantly, educators or their advocates can sometimes assume that students *should* be interested in the content they teach because of its inherent or contextually specific value. The problem of inherent value is easy to address and challenge, but that of contextually specific value is more complicated to unpick. The contextually specific value of certain educational products is often determined by a version of the argument that: *this educational product will be useful at certain specified or unspecified personal or social junctures.* A quick conversation with almost any person who has undergone a formal education reveals quite how little of the content they have supposedly 'learned' they actually recall or find any value for in their lives. The solution that is often provided to this educationally produced problem is that contemporary mass education is the issue and should be improved or replaced by an alternative practice which provides a more substantial, or 'real,' education. Perhaps though, this itself is a solution being posed to a false problem, where it is rather the very idea of compulsory educational imposition that should be in question, not whatever specific form it might take.

Resisting inheritance

Most justifications for obligatory education rely upon an *if x then y* conditional logic that is already caught up in external processes of legitimation, and further if/then conceits. The most simplistic but also prolific of these is perhaps: *if* you want a 'good' job *then* you must study 'successfully.' Such formulations can also be reversed: *if* you study 'successfully,' *then* you will (be more likely to) get a 'good' job. However, as this example indicates, more caveats must be employed if the action precedes the consequence, because while the action is often necessary for the consequence, the consequence is not necessarily brought about by the action. The implications of this dissymmetrical reversibility are significant in an educational context, particularly if the latter formulation obscures or elides its caveat, so as to (falsely) enhance its own procedural legitimacy. Obligatory education, thus, in the act of reinforcing its legitimacy, 'inevitably polarizes a society; it also grades the nations of the world according to an institutional caste system.'[10] This social polarisation and global caste system is itself legitimated by the logic of education's redemptive, corrective, and progressive power.

These primary legitimations do not prescribe a particular form of education, but they frame many discourses and practices of educational intention, allowing secondary if/then legitimations to be protected. The content of any particular syllabus or curriculum might not directly refer to this primary legitimation, but it will nonetheless be 'insured' by it. There are many other primary legitimations that act as motors for more specific educational intentions, including those related to parental influence and social stigma. Equally, the notion of 'being educated' is often co-opted by secondary legitimations, without the need to rely on other logics. More often than not, though, this notion is appended to other primary legitimations. The question of whether or not a particular course of study provides such an education is offset by the backwards projection of a vague but powerful conception of what it means to be educated and why it is important.

Of course, not all obligatory educational processes rely on these specific legitimations. Legitimation can be offered in the name of, for example: emancipation, social justice, interest, or entertainment. Different legitimations can overlap, or help to provide grounds for one another. Equally, teachers operating within highly ordered education systems can countermand, undermine, or reconfigure national or institutional intentions, thereby transgressing or limiting the influence of their legitimations, even as those legitimations might, intentionally or not, support their capacity to do so. Transgressions, also, might be conducted in the very name of another type of justified and legitimated education, as far as the teacher is concerned. Neither compliance nor subversion is neutral: 'There is no neutral or natural place in teaching.'[11]

Obligatory education involves decisions (often at many levels) on curriculum and pedagogy – even if there is no set curriculum or if it is framed as an emancipatory pedagogy – and these decisions are likely to be somewhat informed by processes of legitimation. What is taught and how it is taught cannot be based on neutral decisions because the value of the consequences implied in the conditional if/then structures of legitimation must be affirmed before secondary legitimations can proceed. Must we know why we are doing it before we proceed, either as teacher or as student? What is it that makes the answer to the question 'why?' satisfactory or unsatisfactory? Why does *this* consequence matter enough for *this* action? And is the inferred means to the consequence the only or best means to meet that consequence? Explicit or implicit responses to questions such as these produce the rules that underpin widespread as well as less common educational practices.

A problem pointed to by Maurice Blanchot is that we often follow such rules and ultimately illegitimate structures of legitimation willingly, paradoxically even when they suppress the very rights that law is considered to exist for:

> Rules also suppress the rights which go along with the notion of law, and establish the reign of pure procedure which – a manifestation of technical competence, of sheer knowledge – invests everything, controls everything, submits every gesture to its administration, so that there is no longer any possibility of liberation, for one can no longer speak of oppression.[12]

While many of the 'rules' common to contemporary educational theories and practices are inherited and based on historical processes of legitimation, this does not mean they are (or ever were) just or fit for purpose. Conversely, the practical implications of a complete overhaul or the designing of alternative systems or institutions, as well as aspects of what currently exists that might be considered worth preserving, cannot be ignored when deliberating alternatives. As Samir Haddad puts it:

> One has no option but to keep legacies alive when inheriting them. This also means that the act of reaffirmation of a legacy is not chosen. All heirs reaffirm what they inherit, for none can avoid keeping a legacy alive, even when what is strived for is to put it to death. Such an attempt will always fail. Reaffirmation is thus a necessity, in the sense of necessarily pertaining to all acts of inheritance.[13]

By this logic, the very attempt to put to death the humanist legacy in education is destined to fail, at least in the short term, not least because the resources drawn upon, and the context within which this book is written is to a greater or lesser extent circumscribed by it and result in its perpetuation. That said, resistance to theories or practices of education is not inaction. By resisting the theoretical or practical imposition of overbearing, positivistic educational norms and expectations, as well as resisting claims that solutions to societies' problems, are necessarily educational, education can be reframed. On the one hand, as an activity or experience that is not necessarily 'good,' even (or perhaps especially) in its ideal form; on the other, as inclusive of dissonant educational experiences that might sometimes confound us and which cannot be premeditated by others. Resisting the legitimating narratives and technologies of educational oppressions that claim to save or redeem us does not mean we can or, given contemporary circumstances, would want to fully escape them. However, it might provide the distance and language to criticise them, as well as purportedly 'progressive' alternatives which nonetheless seek to quell resistance once and for all. It might also provide tools to imagine social relations less fettered by the logic of the humanist educational legacy.

Resistance to education is, first of all, the very fact of dissonant educational experience which exceeds dominant instructional forms of educational imposition: it is an education *against* or *outside* social, institutionalised, 'individualising' education. Resistance to the education of social order, though, can also be a practice, an activity that questions the legitimacy of every educational oppression, even, and perhaps especially, if that oppression claims to redeem or save us. In this sense, resistance to education is both normative and descriptive, exhibiting features of José Medina's 'epistemology of resistance,' for whom, '[resistance] can feel more like being pulled in different directions from the inside, like being torn from within. Experiencing resistance can often be like feeling a rupture that one does not know what to do with (at least initially), like feeling perplexity.'[14] Haddad's negotiation of inheritance theorises a similar rupture; for him a disjuncture, where 'A call for justice may well resound from the disjuncture of time, and one can indeed move in this aporia, sorting through the legacies that are bequeathed from the past. But this movement will never be made with the assurance of its being just.'[15] Thus, even in the name of resistance, the negotiated inheritance of educational forms, while momentarily taking leave from legitimation, must make a provisional return to its logic to be able to decide. As Jean-François Lyotard puts it:

> between statements that narrate or describe something and statements that prescribe something, there is always some talking to be done. There is a change of language game. One describes a model of strategy, of society, of economy, and then, when one passes to prescriptions, one has jumped into another language game. One is without criteria, yet one must decide.[16]

Such decisions are perhaps particularly urgent under conditions of epistemic oppression – which are, it could be argued, omnipresent in institutional educational contexts and societies that legitimate and are legitimated by them – so, for Medina, there is

> [an] obligation to resist that leads to many epistemic duties: to fight against ignorance, to know oneself and others in certain respects, to learn and to facilitate the learning of others, to resist epistemic vices and to work towards epistemic virtues, to meliorate epistemic habits and attitudes, and in short, to collaborate in the pursuit of epistemic justice.[17]

Discerning and acting for epistemic justice, though, as Medina makes clear, is hardly straightforward. For this reason he argues that 'if our normative theories should start where we are, in media res, we should start our theorizing by reflecting on the details of the actual injustices that surround us, rather than by speculating about what perfect justice should be. We need a *theory of injustice* more than a theory of justice.'[18] Focusing on the latter rather than the former contributes 'to the invisibility of everyday injustices, to the formation of active bodies of ignorance that perpetuate the injustices and desensitize us to the suffering they cause.'[19] To combat this, Medina advocates for 'resistant imaginations' that 'work both retrospectively and prospectively,' and can be seen to negotiate inheritances, which, I would claim, are always somewhat educational inheritances. For Medina, 'Our imaginings can be conformist or resistant when they look back into our past, when they look forward into our future, when they look around in our present, and when they look sideways into alternative realities.'[20] Our imaginings might then help us to constitute, as Deleuze puts it, real rather than false problems.

Utility

Resistant imagination can take many forms in the context of education, especially as a theory of unjust education or the injustices of education. The efforts of this book, to some extent, attempt to employ what Medina calls a resistant imagination, directed against but also outside the dominant myths, theories, and practices of education. This is not in the service of any particular alternative to intentional, compulsory education. It certainly does not advocate for any educational policy, not least because, as David Graeber suggests:

> The notion of 'policy' presumes a state or governing apparatus which imposes its will on others. 'Policy' is the negation of politics; policy is by definition something concocted by some form of elite, which presumes it knows better than other how their affairs are to be conducted. By participating in policy debates the very best one can achieve is to limit the damage, since the very premise is inimical to the idea of people managing their own affairs.[21]

By this logic, education policy and policy-guided education negate politics. Both within restricted, oppressive contexts, and contexts freer from such educational violence, knowledge and approaches have been and can be developed that do not pretend to be of any significance universally or even beyond their specific context, and thus do not require policy or the negation of politics, either generally or specifically in relation to education. James C. Scott revives a form of partisan knowledge allergic to such policy-based initiatives: mētis, from a tradition of Ancient Greek thought that is utterly opposed to the 'top-down' approach to philosophy, politics, and education that is promoted in the *Republic*, inherited by the humanists and passed down into compulsory education:

> We might reasonably think of situated, local knowledge as being *partisan* knowledge as opposed to generic knowledge. That is, the holder of such knowledge typically has a passionate interest in a particular outcome. An insurer of commercial shipping for a large, highly capitalized maritime firm can afford to rely on probability distributions for accidents. But for a sailor or captain hoping for a safe voyage, it is the outcome of a single event, a single trip that matters. Mētis is the ability and experience necessary to influence the outcome – to improve the odds – in a particular instance.[22]

In terms of thinking about the practice of educators, this has something in common with Wilfred Carr's notion of a practical philosophy of education that 'is not theoretically justified propositional knowledge but reflectively acquired self-knowledge. So understood it is always an exercise in self-understanding that, by having the potential to transform practitioners understanding of their practice, has the potential to transform practice as well.'[23] While Carr's arguments are framed in the context of contemporary public education, they also hint at a mode of thinking about educational relations that exceed policy, hierarchy, and imposition. Carr might also agree with Scott, that 'Some forms of mētis are disappearing every day. As physical mobility, commodity markets, formal education, professional specialisation, and mass media spread to even the most remote communities, the social conditions for the elaboration of mētis are undermined.'[24] Important, also, is that 'mētis does not put all its eggs in one basket; it makes no claim to universality and in this sense is pluralistic.'[25] Mētis, also, can be the practical result of a non-compulsory and even non-intentional education.

Those that exhibit mētis in a particular area of life do not require the legitimation of credentialisation or the authority of the state to support their authority of competence. In many contexts, individuals can gain from accepting the authority of competence that certain other individuals, who may or may not explicitly be educators, might deserve. This could just as well be a plumber as a specialist in nineteenth-century literature; although the former might be relied on to perform, or teach how to perform, a task because of their competence, the latter's speculations on their area of expertise might be of particular interest to those wanting to learn about that specific area. Nonetheless, the authority of competence is a convoluted subject in the context of education, for two main reasons: (1) it often relies on imposed authority rather than accepted authority, (2) authority is claimed or accepted in subjects/areas that are culturally validated but, when scrutinised, may be masquerading as much more necessary or significant to the living of a (desirable or decent enough) life than they actually are. The legitimacy of our dominant practices of education, inherited from humanism, does not usually rely on individual judgements about the competence of those who we choose, or, more often, do not choose, to be educated by. This is not to suggest that the majority of teachers are incompetent at what they are required to do; quite to the contrary, they are perhaps all too competent in forms of education where 'pure procedure' reigns.[26] It is rather that their authority comes from a long-standing social and educational inheritance that takes as its prerequisite that we must be educated in a particular way to be full members of society, and that our material conditions and our place in social hierarchies will be 'legitimately' determined in part by that education. Rather than be educated by or alongside those who we choose, based on our needs, interests, and judgements about their competence or mētis in a particular area, we are educated for the majority of our childhood, and in many cases, significant portions of our adulthood, by those whose primary competence is in *education*. It is a self-closing loop, legitimated and expanded over centuries by its top-down imposition.

What is required, then, is not a better philosophy of education to guide us or a better set of educational policies but rather, on the one hand, a concerted deflation of the humanist legacy in education, most notably in its inheritance as the ever-expanding field of policy-driven formal educational intervention, especially in its compulsory or quasi-compulsory form. By quasi-compulsory, I refer to the way in which, especially tertiary, education has, for many, become a socially and economically 'necessary' activity. On the other hand, plural forms of partisan approaches to educational experience and practice must be preserved and initiated because the legitimacy of the dominant imposed forms of education is untenable. Their legitimacy relies on the logic of 'lack,' in the sense that education is intended to provide something that is significantly wanting in individuals or communities. Echoing Ivan Illich, Gustavo Esteva, Madhu S. Prakash, and Dana L. Stuchol describe this situation:

> All of the caring, disabling professions are presented as a 'cure' for a deficiency, lack, or need that the professional service can best satisfy. Modern living has now become so dependent on such services that it is rarely perceived how they have transformed traditional sufficiency into the need they supposedly satisfy. Modern needs are not born out of necessities, as human limitations are defined in traditional societies. Modern needs are created through forms of deprivation and destitution, which reorganize the society and redefine the human condition.[27]

This is, as should be obvious, no call for 'better' educators. They rather attempt to see the education system for what it is: a system that constructs its own sense of 'need' and thereby the basis of its own internal educational economy, which is itself a component of larger state capitalist economies that rely significantly on the exponential construction of need and scarcity. Forming another intersection with what, in the previous chapter, we saw Pierre Klossowski call a 'monstrous hypertrophy' of 'needs' and Georges Batille describe as 'unproductive expenditure,' Esteva, Prakash, and Stuchol's Ilichian inference that the educator is a caring but also disabling professional is apt because of its construction and imposition of a non-pre-existing lack on its subjects. This could be seen almost as contempt for the learner. Hardly an attack on learning itself, their approach is a critique grounded in a similar manner to that of the anarchist theorist, Colin Ward, for whom, 'The anarchist approach to learning is grounded, not in a contempt for learning, but in a respect for the learner.'[28] The prospective learner, though, for Esteva, Prakash, and Stuchol, often sees through the market-creating propaganda of educational economies:

> While the educated persist in their competitive struggle to consume more knowledge, the uneducated or undereducated are weaning themselves of the secular faith in such dependency. Confronted by the propaganda of knowledge peddling, they adopt the same attitude that they take before junk food: They know that the latter does not nourish, although sometimes it may curb hunger. They realize that education, akin to junk food, is unable to generate communal wisdom or to guide experience.[29]

For Ward, there is even an opportunity resting in this disenfranchisement:

> The likeliest lever for change in the organised system will come, not from criticism or example from outside but from pressure from below. There has always been a proportion of pupils who attend unwillingly, who resent the authority of the school and its arbitrary regulations, and who put a low value on the processes of education because their own experience tells them that it is an obstacle race in which they are so often the losers that they would be mugs to enter the competition. *This* is what school has taught them, and when this army of also-rans, no longer cowed by threats, no longer amenable to cajolery, no longer to be bludgeoned by physical violence into sullen acquiescence grows large enough to prevent the school from functioning with even the semblance of relevance or effectiveness, the educational revolution will begin.[30]

The legitimacy of education is sustained in significant part by its omnipresence and 'necessity.' In this sense, it is remarkable precisely because it is often its own justification. Its legitimacy strikes from many sides: its legal compulsions, its social expectations, and its multifaceted performative necessities in selection for employment. These legitimacies are themselves underpinned by the supposed legitimacy of the state, of state-capitalist economies, and of their concomitant social organisation and control. There are, of course, an ever-growing number of critiques of neoliberal economics and its effects. Many of its critics blame (an often vague conception of) neoliberalism for tainting education. The education that has been tainted is often understood nostalgically and is reliant on a certain conservative humanism. Among these critiques, notably those from anarchist perspectives, there are those that go further and justifiably put into question the very legitimacy of the state and, implicitly, its educational policies. However, as we have seen, even many of these more radical and credible critics of both state-capitalism and the state itself either do not concern themselves with education to any great degree or else propose compulsory or quasi-compulsory alternatives that rely on particular forms of policy, practice, and a conception of the educated person that does not stray too far from the humanist legacy.

Notes

1 Ivan Illich, *Deschooling Society* (London: Marion Boyars, 1971), 38–44.
2 Ibid., 38.
3 Pierre Bourdieu and Jean-Claude Passeron, *Reproduction in Education, Society and Culture*, trans. Richard Nice (London: Sage, 1990), 206.
4 Peter Gelderloos, *Anarchy Works: Examples of Anarchist Ideas in Practice* (London: što čitaš, 2018), 75.
5 Gilles Deleuze, *Bergsonism*, trans. Hugh Tomlinson and Barbara Habberjam (New York: Zone Books, 1991), 15.

6 Michel Foucault, *Discipline and Punish,* trans. Alan Sheridan (London: Penguin, 1991), 186–187.

7 Deleuze, *Bergsonism,* 98.

8 Gilles Deleuze, *Difference and Repetition,* trans. Paul Patton (London: Continuum, 2004), 260.

9 Deleuze, *Bergsonism,* 98.

10 Illich, *Deschooling Society,* 9.

11 Jacques Derrida, *Who's Afraid of Philosophy?: Right to Philosophy 1,* trans. Jan Plug (Stanford, CA: Stanford University Press, 2002), 69.

12 Maurice Blanchot, *The Writing of the Disaster,* trans. Ann Smock (Lincoln, NE: University of Nebraska Press, 1986), 144.

13 Samir Haddad, *Derrida and the Inheritance of Democracy* (Bloomington: Indiana University Press, 2013), 32.

14 José Medina, *The Epistemology of Resistance: Gender and Racial Oppression, Epistemic Injustice, and Resistant Imaginations* (Oxford: Oxford University Press, 2013), p. 16.

15 Haddad, *Derrida and the Inheritance of Democracy,* 44.

16 Jean-François Lyotard and Jean-Loup Thébaud, *Just Gaming,* trans. Brian Massumi (Manchester: Manchester University Press, 1985), 17.

17 Medina, *The Epistemology of Resistance,* 16–17.

18 Ibid., 12.

19 Ibid., 13.

20 Ibid., 299.

21 David Graeber, *Fragments of an Anarchist Anthropology* (Chicago, IL: Prickly Paradigm Press, 2004), 9.

22 James C. Scott, *Seeing Like a State: How Certain Schemes to Improve the Human Condition Have Failed* (New Haven, CT: Yale University Press, 1998), 318.

23 Wilfred Carr, 'Philosophy And Education—A Symposium,' *Journal of Philosophy of Education* 39: 4 (2005), 625.

24 Scott, *Seeing Like a State,* 335.

25 Ibid., 340.

26 Blanchot, *The Writing of the Disaster,* 144.

27 Gustavo Esteva, Dana Lynn Stuchul, and Madhu Suri Prakash, 'From a Pedagogy for Liberation to Liberation from Pedagogy' in *Rethinking Freire: Globalization and the Environmental Crisis,* eds. Chet A. Bowers and Frederique Apffel-Marglin (London: Routledge, 2015), 17–18.

28 Colin Ward, *Anarchy in Action* (Oakland, CA: PM Press, 2018), 97.

29 Esteva et al., 28.

30 Ward, *Anarchy in Action,* 97–98.

Part II

Outside

Chapter 6

Psyche

Provisional weapons and rhetorical tools

Introducing the relevance of Sigmund Freud's definitions of primary and secondary narcissism – as well as the ego, id, and super-ego/ego ideal – to understandings of educational experience, this short chapter provides the psychoanalytic language that will be read alongside Virginia Woolf's *The Waves* in the next chapter, as well as the Blanchotian and Derridean notions of narcissism in Chapter 8. Woolf's novel and Derrida's and Blanchot's various texts both illustrate and frustrate these educationally significant components of Freud's psychic economy. I do not turn to Freud's terminology and theoretical framework out of adherence to his psychoanalytic principles or their scientific veracity (in fact, I would describe his findings as being at least as symptomatic of the humanist legacy as they are diagnostic) but because, as Derrida put it in conversation with Élisabeth Roudinesco, 'the very aim, and I do say the *aim,* of the psychoanalytic revolution is the only one not to rest, not to seek refuge, in principle, in what I call a theological or humanist alibi'[1] and, within that context,

> the id, the ego, the super ego, the ideal ego, the ego ideal, the secondary process and the primary process of repression, etc. – in a word, the large Freudian machines (including the concept and the word 'unconscious'!) – are in my opinion only provisional weapons, or even rhetorical tools cobbled together to be used against a philosophy of consciousness, of transparent and fully responsible intentionality.[2]

As such, I read Freud in the same way that I go on to read other unfaithful inheritors of the humanist legacy, as means to the development of provisional weapons and rhetorical tools for use against that legacy and its more faithful adherents.

Psychic economy

In Freud's understanding, underpinning all ego formation is 'the great reservoir of libido' called the id.[3] The id is the ego's 'second external world, which it strives to bring into subjection to itself. It withdraws libido from the id and transforms object-cathexes of the id into ego-structures.'[4] This is why, for Freud, the ego is

> a poor creature owing service to three masters and consequently menaced by three dangers: from the external world, from the libido of the id, and from the severity of the super-ego. Three kinds of anxiety correspond to these three dangers, since anxiety is the expression of a retreat from danger. As a frontier-creature, the ego tries to mediate between the world and the id, to make the id pliable to the world and, by means of its muscular activity, to make the world fall in with the wishes of the id.[5]

All of these frontiers are, to an extent, also frontiers of educational experience and the education of the psychic economy. Although the ego and the more specific education that is ego formation is central to Freud's thought, the more obviously heterogeneous education of the psychic economy produces the context within which the ego is perpetually formed and deformed. Narcissism is one of the features of the psychic economy to which Freud draws particular attention.

Narcissism, for Freud, is not a perversion but rather 'the libidinal complement to the egoism of the instinct of self-preservation, a measure of which may justifiably be attributed to every living creature.'[6] Freud himself, then, helps to de-pathologise narcissism from the outset in explaining its contribution to *all* ego formation and preservation. For him,

> a unity comparable to the ego cannot exist in the individual form from the start; the ego has to be developed. The auto-erotic instincts, however, are there from the very first; so there must be something added to auto-erotism – a new psychical action – in order to bring about narcissism.[7]

This new psychical action involves a 'departure from primary narcissism' due to the 'displacement of libido on to an ego ideal imposed from without.'[8] Primary narcissism is exhibited in the original auto-erotism, whereas secondary narcissism comes later and contributes to the formation of the ego:

> At the very beginning, all the libido is accumulated in the id, while the ego is still in the process of formation or is still feeble. The id sends part of this libido out into erotic object-cathexes, whereupon the ego, now grown stronger, tried to get hold of this object-libido and to force itself on the id as love object. The narcissism of the ego is thus a secondary one, which has been withdrawn from objects.[9]

This secondary narcissism is the id's replacement for the primary narcissism experienced in childhood. What follows the introduction of secondary narcissism is an impossible but 'vigorous attempt to recover' the auto-erotic state of primary narcissism through fulfilment of what Freud calls the ego ideal. Here, already, an educational logic is at play in ego formation; the ego ideal representing the psychic internalisation of the educational influence of external forces, such as parents, teachers, friends, and communities, as well as experience more broadly.

The ideal ego (or super-ego) 'is the substitute for the lost narcissism of his childhood in which he was his own ideal.'[10] The super-ego is, like the ego, not only the concoction of external forces, but the partial co-option of the libido's cathectic energy by those, often educational, forces:

> it is impossible for the super-ego as for the ego to disclaim its origin from things heard; for it is a part of the ego and remains accessible to consciousness by way of these word-presentations (concepts, abstractions). But the *cathectic energy* does not reach these contents of the super-ego from auditory perception (instruction or reading) but from sources in the id.[11]

However, at the same time as the libido is displaced on to the ego ideal, 'libidinal object-cathexes' are also sent out, in service of the id, the ego becoming 'impoverished in favour of these cathexes, just as it does in favour of the ego ideal,' and thereby also enriched and satisfied 'in respect of the object, just as it does by fulfilling its ideal.'[12] These libidinally informed experiences produce three forms of self-regard, the first of which is 'the residue of infantile narcissism,' the second arises from the 'omnipotence' of the ego ideal and its fulfilment, which has been formed by experience, while the 'third part proceeds from the satisfaction of object-libido.'[13] However, this latter form of self-regard has 'severe conditions' imposed upon it by the ego ideal, meaning that 'some of them [are] to be rejected by means of its censor, as being incompatible.'[14]

This censoring function of the ego ideal, whose formation, again, is understood as being significantly and intentionally influenced externally by explicitly and implicitly educational forces, has drastic consequences for the libido and, ultimately, the ego. Freud explains that 'libidinal instinctual impulses undergo the vicissitude of pathogenic repression if they come into conflict with the subject's cultural and ethical ideas.'[15] The formation of an ego ideal, thanks in significant part to external educational influence, 'would be the conditioning factor of repression.'[16] Freud suggests that 'It would not surprise us if we were to find a special psychical agency which performs the task of seeing that narcissistic satisfaction from the ego ideal is ensured and which, with this end in view, constantly watches the actual ego and measures it by that ideal.'[17] This special psychical agency, for Freud, explains the phenomenon of feeling like we are 'being *watched*.'[18] He has no doubt that such a 'complaint is justified; it describes the truth. A power of this kind, watching, discovering and criticizing all our intentions, does really exist. Indeed, it exists in every one of us in normal life.'[19] This watchman is a psychic implant, principally facilitated during our education and its co-option of the libidinal energy of the id:

> For what prompted the subject to form an ego ideal, on whose behalf his conscience acts as watchman, arose from the critical influence of his parents (conveyed to him by the medium of the voice), to whom were added, as time went on, those who trained and taught him and the innumerable and indefinable host of all the other people in his environment – his fellow-men – and public opinion.[20]

In Freud's understanding it is clear that education plays a significant part in shaping the psyche, especially in its cathectic co-option of libidinal energy attached to the super-ego's educationally informed character. At the same time, though, that education, in its broadest sense, forms the ego, both through object-cathexes and what might be called a super-ego-cathexes, a much more delimited form of specific education-cathexes can take place that seems to incorporate both object-cathexes and super-ego-cathexes.

While this process is complex and always individualised, it is nonetheless possible to outline its most prominent features. On the one hand, aspects of what is commonly described as education, usually in the context of schooling or higher education, capture the libido's cathectic energy in the form of object-cathexes, meaning that certain aspects of formal and intentional education provide unquestionable pleasure (perhaps a particular subject, text, or activity). On the other hand, and overlapping in a tangled manner with these object-cathexes, particular formulations of educational success and an idealisation of an educated persona take hold in the super-ego. This latter effect is not necessarily *at all* influenced by object-cathexes, in the sense that these idealisations may not cohere with the pleasures experienced in undertaking particular educational activities. Of course, in pursuit of the fulfilment of the ideal, contexts may arise where the more direct pleasures of object-cathexes are also possible, but the purpose of the ideal is not pleasure, it is (self-) control. Equally, the ideal may not remain at all stable, even if its basic structure of idealising a particular version of oneself as a type of educated person does, alongside the punishment of oneself for failing to achieve (always somewhat imposed) notions of educational success. In the light of its idealisations, the super-ego punishes the ego for its transgressions, and the non-idealised pleasures that the id seeks, with the help of the ego, are more likely to be consciously rejected or repressed. Freud argues that 'From the point of view of instinctual control, of morality, it may be said of the id that it is totally non-moral, of the ego that it strives to be moral, and of the super-ego that it can be super-moral and then become as cruel as only the id can be.'[21] This cruelty takes hold in childhood and continues into adulthood, often in the service of specifically educational ideals and standards of achievement. The cruel structure of this imposed and socially validated educational logic runs on a disposition of humility and a sense of guilt:

> The self-judgement which declares that the ego falls short of its ideal produces the religious sense of humility to which the believer appeals in his longing. As a child grows up, the role of father is carried on by teachers and others in authority; their injunctions and prohibitions remain powerful in the ego ideal and continue, in the form of conscience, to exercise the moral censorship. The tension between the demands of *conscience* and the actual performances of the ego is experienced as a *sense of guilt*.[22]

This humility and guilt fundamentally supports a deference to a social hierarchy upheld in significant part by educational stratification. Of course there are many – notably those who have not benefited from it and have not seen it benefit their families or communities – who reject the legitimacy of this educational logic and its concomitant hierarchy, however, their critique is considered illegitimate by the educated, blinkered by their reverence.

Obedience

There are those committed to education who are nonetheless critical of its already existing hierarchies, and who may even be critical of social hierarchy altogether, the problem being that their solutions often either tend to be based on creating an equally committed and oppressive largely uniform compulsory education for everyone or in cutting off a small piece of this educational logic, enhancing it in an alternative way, sometimes explicitly in egalitarian forms but nonetheless productive of a particular desirable educational persona that is somehow more authentic than its counterparts in the broader educational logic they reject. This latter critique even extends to advocates of home-schooling, who also, in spite of protecting children from the dominant educational logic's primary manifestation in the school, like some alternative schools, cannot at all feasibly protect them from its effects in many aspects of their social lives. There might, at root in all proposed and practiced substitutes for mainstream schooling, lie the same humility and guilt directed towards education as the most conformist of educational institutions and its subjects: a sense of humility towards a more 'authentic' education and a sense of guilt for not having accessed it sufficiently for oneself, one's students, or one's children. As a counterpoint to this guilt, though, lies the (secondary) narcissistic pride in having sufficiently subjected oneself to these idealised demands.

Unlike the unpleasure, as Freud calls it, caused by having to renounce ones instincts for explicitly external reasons, 'obedience to the super-ego,' as internal reason, 'has a different economic effect.'[23] While renunciation in obedience to the super-ego can still cause unpleasure 'it also brings the ego a yield of pleasure – a substitutive satisfaction, as it were. The ego feels elevated; it is proud of the instinctual renunciation, as though it were a valuable achievement.'[24] This yield of pleasure is thanks to the super-ego's historic co-option of the libido's cathectic energy. Adherence to historically imposed educational means and ends, even, and perhaps especially, when resulting in the renunciation of the pleasures of object-cathexes, creates its own form of pleasure in pride:

> The super-ego is the successor and representative of the individual's parents (and educators) who had supervised his actions in the first period of his life; it carries on their functions almost unchanged. It keeps the ego in a permanent state of dependence and exercises a constant pressure on it. Just as in childhood, the ego is apprehensive about risking the love of its supreme master; it feels his approval as liberation and satisfaction and his reproaches as pangs of conscience. When the ego has brought the super-ego the sacrifice of an instinctual renunciation, it expects to be rewarded by receiving more love from it. The consciousness of deserving this love is felt by it as pride. At the time when the authority had not yet been internalized as a super-ego, there could be the same relation between the threat of loss of love and the claims of instinct: there was a feeling of security and satisfaction when one had achieved an instinctual renunciation out of love for one's parents. But this happy feeling could only assume the peculiar narcissistic character of pride after the authority had itself become a portion of the ego.[25]

For Freud the ego ideal is 'the heir of the Oedipus complex, and thus it is also the expression of the most powerful impulses and most important libidinal vicissitudes of the id.'[26] The Oedipus complex, though, is itself the product of authoritarian social formation, its 'delegated agent': the family.[27] For Deleuze and Guattari, desire is not Oedipal, rather, 'it is the social repression of desire or sexual repression – that is, the *stasis* of libidinal energy – that actualizes Oedipus and engages desire in this requisite impasse, organized by the repressive society.'[28]

> Psychic repression is such that social repression becomes desired; it induces a consequent desire, a faked image of its object, on which it bestows the appearance of independence. Strictly speaking, psychic repression is a means in the service of social repression: desiring production. But it in fact implies an original double operation: the repressive social formation delegates its power to an agent of psychic repression, and correlatively the repressed desire is as though masked by the faked displaced image to which the repression gives rise. Psychic repression is delegated by the social formation, while the desiring formation is disfigured, displaced by psychic repression.[29]

As such, we read Freud in the context of the ongoing reality of these social repressions and their psychic counterparts, understanding his theoretical formulations, not as interpretations of underlying and somewhat universal human nature, but as a limited kind of psychic anthropology of his own society, itself a symptom of the repressions it intended to analyse. Whether or not Freud was as unaware of this symptomatic aspect of his own thought is perhaps not as clear as Deleuze and Guattari imply in *Anti-Oedipus*, they do bring it to the fore.

Notes

1 Jacques Derrida and Elisabeth Roudinesco, *For What Tomorrow: A Dialogue*, trans. Jeff Fort (Stanford, CA: Stanford University Press, 2004), 173.
2 Derrida and Roudinesco, *For What Tomorrow*, 172.
3 Sigmund Freud, 'The Ego and The Id,' in *On Metapsychology* (Harmondsworth: Penguin, 1991), 369, n. 1.
4 Ibid., 397.
5 Ibid., 397–398.
6 Sigmund Freud, 'On Narcissism' in Sigmund Freud,' *On Metapsychology* (Harmondsworth: Penguin, 1991), 66.
7 Ibid., 69.
8 Ibid., 95.
9 Freud, 'The Ego and The Id,' 387.
10 Freud, 'On Narcissism,' 88.
11 Freud, 'The Ego and The Id,' 394.
12 Freud, 'On Narcissism,' 95.
13 Ibid., 95.
14 Ibid., 95.
15 Ibid., 87.
16 Ibid., 88.
17 Ibid., 89.
18 Ibid., 90.
19 Ibid., 90.
20 Ibid., 90.
21 Freud, 'The Ego and The Id,' 395.
22 Ibid., 376–377.
23 Sigmund Freud, 'Moses and Monotheism,' *The Origins of Religion* (Harmondsworth: Penguin, 1985), 364.
24 Ibid., 364.
25 Ibid., 364.
26 Freud, 'The Ego and The Id,' 376.
27 Gilles Deleuze and Felix Guattari, *Anti-Oedipus: Capitalism and Schizophrenia*, trans. Robert Hurley, Mark Seem, and Helen R. Lane (London: The Athlone Press, 1984), 119.
28 Ibid., 118.
29 Ibid., 119.

Chapter 7

Waves

(De)formation

In this chapter I present Virginia Woolf's *The Waves* as an extraordinary exposition of the education of the psychic economy through what Freud describes as ego formation and prefigures what, with the help of Derrida, the following chapter describes as the formation of form and stabilisation of the non-stable subject.[1] The educational experiences presented in *The Waves* are descriptive rather than prescriptive, and Woolf explores what does happen rather than what should happen. However, despite Woolf's lack of prescription, her insight into what can be understood as parallel to the complex relation between the id, the ego, the super-ego, and the external world allows her readers access to incidences of educational experience ordinarily hidden from them, at least in descriptive terms. To learn about the education of the psychic economy in *The Waves* is to become better equipped for understanding the breadth and variety of educational experience.

In one of the few contemporary analyses of *The Waves*, Maureen Chun argues that 'consciousness is radically depersonalized and physicalized in the novel.'[2] While I agree that there is always an element of depersonalising and physicalising of consciousness in the novel, I contest that consciousness in fact becomes more personal and less physical within the first few pages of the novel and then progressively throughout. This progression can be described as charting the ego's (de)formation in the education of psychic economies. My argument is not laid out explicitly in terms of the unconscious, but it does attempt to account for and respond to the id's libidinal energy and experiences which exceed and effect on ego formation or even simply intentional thought. The id and the progressive co-option of its libidinal energy by the super-ego would seem to determine aspects of individuals which remain constant and might affect behaviours and responses to experiences in sometimes predictable ways.

Misapprehension

Through the different protagonists of *The Waves* (who will be met in the readings below), Woolf provides six examples of the different ways in which these conditions play out. The novel is divided into nine sections, the first three of which are dedicated, in chronological order, to the childhood, youth, and young adulthood of its six protagonists. The novel's complex narrative structure does not easily lend itself to brief synopsis, as the six characters' individual narratives move further apart from one another as the novel progresses. Maurice Blanchot even went so far as to say of the novel that 'plot is not only of no importance, it is imperceptible.'[3] He makes this specific claim in the context of a broader argument on the paradoxes of the novel as an aesthetic form, where he argues that

> novelists have no reason to think that a novel is good just because the plot is well handled or the heroes come from the normal world. On the contrary, a novelist must beware of the easy options provided by imitation, as well as the false resources of character analysis, psychology, or social history. It is within himself, in his inner dream, that he can best reach the mysterious reality whose revelation can only take place in the novel.[4]

Following Blanchot, instead of offering plot summary and character outlines, or relying on Woolf's own psychological motivations, I will move on from my introduction to the basic structure of the novel, and simply gesture towards my close reading of the text, which is where I attempt to come into proximity with the novel's revelation of Woolf's 'mysterious reality.' There is no single story, but rather six, sometimes interrelated, presentations of thought. The first three sections of the novel are the focus of this chapter as they provide its most useful examples of the education of the psychic economy. I will argue that these sections of *The Waves* illustrate how the libidinal energy of an individual's id and its co-option by the super-ego underpins much of the education of their psychic economy. Even though each individual's id plays a significant part in conditioning their education, they are not themselves educable or changeable; only their effects on the super-ego and ego. The id and the libidinal energy it cathects on objects and the super-ego, in Freudian theory, and also in how I interpret it in the context of reading *The Waves*, is not another name for an 'essential self' but rather one of many relations affecting the conscious comprehension, agency, and passive receptivity of self that, for a few of the characters, is often in question. The structure of experience for these individuals is at the educative intersection of their id, their ego, super-ego, and the external world. The experience of this intersection changes who they are, consciously but seemingly also unintentionally, as well as educating the very ego that enables them to conceive of themselves critically *as* a self through the work of the super-ego. Crucially, this 'self' is a site of mobile relationality, correspondent with Leo Bersani's definition, whereby, 'Relationality is grounded in antagonism and misapprehension, which means that to meet the world is always to see the world as a place where I am not – or, if I am there, it is as alienated and/or unrecognizable being.'[5]

The reading I provide here offers less of an opportunity for educators, than an indication of a limit. The implicit claim might then be that there is only so much that can be done in formal, intentional education; especially given that the dynamics required for the education of the psychic economy resides within the relations produced between and within that very psychic economy and its relation to external experience, often set at quite a (non-physical) 'distance' from more empirically verifiable external factors. Equally, these relations are not necessarily or always actively sought or controlled by the individual children or responsible adults, highlighting a passive dimension to educational experience, revealed in the narratives that follow.

Dispositions

The first section of the novel begins with descriptions of almost entirely passive experiences. There is very little content to the thoughts of the children that could not be described as bluntly perceptual or representative of the basic object-cathexes of the id. They see ('a ring ... a slab of pale yellow ... a globe') and hear ('a sound ... something stamping') but they do not consciously act on what they see or hear.[6] However, their perceptions quickly turn to analogies, allowing their empirical experiences of object-cathexes to become a part of an abstracting consciousness: 'The leaves are gathered round the window like pointed ears,' said Susan.'[7] An overlap between internal psychic economy and external experience is already apparent. Memory allows the children to make these analogies and, as external experiences multiply in number, so do the resources of memory. The children all experience different things, so their memories are different and therefore the analogies they are able to make are also different. More pertinently, though, their object-cathexes, and subsequent super-ego-cathexes are all notably distinct. For Woolf, the complexity of individual consciousness seems to begin not with empirical experience but in the relation of memory to empirical experience through analogy. One of the children, Louis, shows what happens when the libidinal energy of his id and its object-cathexes seems to run contrary to the elicitation of a conscious determination of subjectivity:

> 'Now they have all gone,' said Louis. 'I am alone. They have gone into the house for breakfast, and I am left standing by the wall among the flowers. It is very early, before lessons. Flower after flower is specked on the depths of green. The petals are harlequins. Stalks rise from the black hollows beneath. The flowers swim like fish made of

light upon the dark, green waters. I hold a stalk in my hand. I am the stalk. My roots go down to the depths of the world, through earth dry with brick, and damp earth, through veins of lead and silver. I am all fibre ...'[8]

When left alone he loses his identity to his surroundings and exhibits a kind of return to the pre-egoistic experience of primary narcissism. His self at once disintegrates and is extended to become his context: 'I am the stalk.' However, even this relatively radical experience of depersonalisation is not without the resource of memory, here employed in imagination. The experience is one that Louis desires, preferring to be 'all fibre' over the company of the other children. He hears them calling for him but would prefer to 'be unseen.'[9] He is, in this instance, reminiscent of Narcissus himself, who we will come to in the following chapter. It seems as if his socially and consciously determined subjective self has disintegrated, leaving behind an asocial and experientially extended self: he is the stalk, he is not Louis. This experience is not the realisation of an essential self or an example of a Heideggerian authentic moment but merely one among many examples of where the psychic economy of a subject is inseparable from objects due to the cathectic energy of the libido; or, to put it another way, where notions of insides and outsides become indistinct and arbitrary due to the disempowerment of the super-ego and external forces that would co-opt it and the intentions of the subject for their ends. Louis's experience here is exemplary only in that it reveals the complex relations that – albeit in different ways – condition all external interruptions of the psychic economy without simply reinforcing it. For Louis, this intense experience continues until he is found and kissed by Jinny and 'all is shattered.'[10] This second interruption, this time an interruption of his state of something close to primary narcissism, force him to be re-inaugurated as a self.

A few passages after Louis's experience of being the stalk it becomes clear that the children are now in a school classroom. The reader does not know if minutes or years have passed. The children's streams of consciousness continue to unfold at the unique intersections of their psychic economy and external experience but at the same time it is made clear that their very disposition towards language differs from one another's. Louis's asociality remains, but now becomes bound up in his super-ego, and its internalisation of judgements relating to language, national identity, and the social hierarchy: 'I will not conjugate the verb,' said Louis, 'until Bernard has said it. My father is a banker in Brisbane and I speak with an Australian accent. I will wait and copy Bernard. He is English.'[11] It is now apparent that his fixation on his difference from the others is informed both by his asociality and also by his conscious anxiety provoked by a cruel super-ego, which now starts the process of taking the place of the asocial object-cathexes of his id. But Louis is not the only one who is different. All of the children are also not so much shaped by a shared language as they shape it for themselves; or to be more precise, they colour it and move it:

> 'Those are white words,' said Susan, 'like stones one picks up by the seashore.'
> 'They flick their tails right and left as I speak them,' said Bernard. 'They wag their tails; they flick their tails; they move through the air in flocks, now this way, now that way, moving all together, now dividing, now coming together.'
> 'Those are yellow words, those are fiery words,' said Jinny. 'I should like a fiery dress, a yellow dress, a fulvous dress to wear in the evening.'
> 'Each tense,' said Neville, 'means differently. There is an order in this world; there are distinctions, there are differences in this world, upon whose verge I step. For this is only a beginning.'[12]

Taken together these examples seem to reveal a libidinally informed relation that each child has to the objects of language, which itself shapes their linguistic consciousness of their worlds. Louis, Susan, Bernard, Jinny, and Neville all come to language differently. Language and linguistic consciousness are also the basis of libidinally charged object-relations in *The Waves*. The Latin words the children are reading in class are perceived in part by a non-linguistically conscious aspect of the psychic economy and they are assisted by conscious analogy, through their super-egos, to begin to understand these as linguistically anchored objects which have a meaning at least partly separate to that which they experience intuitively through object-cathexes. The exception to this is Rhoda, for whom written language does not yet *mean* in the same way as language that is spoken or thought. Because she is unable to complete the exercises that the teacher has set, she is held back alone after class:

> The figures mean nothing now. Meaning has gone. The clock ticks. The two hands are convoys marching through a desert. The black bars on the clock face are green oases. The long hand has marched ahead to find water. The other, painfully stumbles among hot stones in the desert. It will die in the desert.[13]

Rhoda's imagination takes flight as the figures on the page continue to mean nothing. While for the other children the written words not only had meaning but unique meaning, libidinally informed by object-cathexes, for Rhoda their non-meaning is an experience in and of itself. The difficulty that the reader is presented with is the decision as to whether or not Rhoda's libidinal disposition prohibits her from engaging with the written words or, instead, if she does not yet have the conscious capacity to understand them. Either way, the education of the psychic economy is key to both increasing the capacity for learning and understanding, as well as to creating a conscious disposition, often through the super-ego's contribution to ego formation, which might counteract or take the place of the disposition brought about by the id.

In the way of experience

In the second section of *The Waves*, the passages recording what I am, with Freud, calling ego formation, grow longer and the language becomes more advanced. In this section, it also becomes clear that Woolf has separated the sections into subsections set into separate periods of time. The beginning of the section is set at the children's first arrival at secondary school, whereas it ends at the start of a summer holiday. The major change in terms of the consciousness of most of the protagonists is that conscious predicates have more thoroughly begun to take the place of the dispositions of their id. The clear disjunction between the libido and ego formation apparent in the first section begins to disappear. This is either because the linguistic consciousness accompanying ego formation, understood as work in service of the super-ego, is more fully able to articulate the dispositions of their id than before or rather, as I argue, that its predicates have begun to co-opt those earlier dispositions. The more capable the children become at thinking in language, the less likely they are to be influenced directly by their libido in object-cathexes. Therefore, even if the initial disposition towards language is predicated by how the id's libidinal energy becomes cathected, the education of linguistic consciousness and the critical capacities of the super-ego, as a part of ego formation, comes at the cost of the pre-linguistic dispositions of the id. Alongside the repression of the id is the reduction of the children's more passive experiences. Their thoughts are consistently directed towards active behaviour or opinionated reflection on experiences they are subjected to. What this section of *The Waves* begins more noticeably to illustrate is how language, or more specifically, ego formation, *gets in the way* of experience. To put it another way, as it develops, the ego becomes an increasingly dominant aspect of experience for the children. Their id is no longer mediated by their thoughts but rather repressed by them in service of the super-ego.

This experience of language and ego formation standing between the id and the world is articulated in different ways by all of the protagonists. Bernard's opening monologue shows that this process is, for him at least, an active form of defence against the emotional experience the world around him provokes on his first day at school: 'I must make phrases and phrases and so interpose something hard between myself and the stare of housemaids, the stare of clocks, staring faces, indifferent faces, or I shall cry.'[14] Language is not only the barrier that exists to stop his tears from flowing, but a barrier between himself and the world. This barrier soon begins to become the most definitive aspect of his self. The same is true for Louis, who experiences the use of language as a means of conveying or creating perceptions of identity, notably in relation to social hierarchy and status. He hears other boys boasting but feels that he cannot join in, '"My uncle is the best shot in England. My cousin is Master of Foxhounds." Boasting begins. And I cannot boast, for my father is a banker in Brisbane, and I speak with an Australian accent.'[15] In the first section of the novel, Louis does not want to speak in class because of this same self-consciousness, and here the repetition of this reticence is striking because it indicates a persistent conscious preoccupation with what he perceives as a hierarchical inadequacy. His concern for the effect his accent will have on how he is perceived reveals additional tensions that can exist between self, language, and world.

For Neville, on the other hand, language is primarily something external, to be learned and enjoyed. When he arrives at the school he sees the library as being, 'where I shall explore the exactitude of the Latin language, and step firmly upon the well-laid sentences, and pronounce the explicit, the sonorous hexameters of Virgil, of Lucretius; and chant with a passion that is never obscure or formless the loves of Catullus, reading from a big book, a quarto with margins.'[16] Although these texts loom large in the humanist canon, his interest seems less to do with self-formation or the development of rhetorical skills than with the singular aesthetic relations he might be able to experience with these texts. Language here is not the language of internal consciousness but rather of 'external' (and therefore desired and desirable) experience, although as the first section of the novel made clear, these distinctions can be relatively arbitrary. Neville, then, has been able to retain his libidinal capacity for object-cathexes related to language through its co-option by the super-ego. The object-cathexes of primary narcissism now have a secondary narcissistic value in their educational contribution. What sets Neville apart from the other two boys is his apparent joy upon arrival at school and his perception of language as something to be enjoyed rather than to be used as a means of asking questions about oneself. Despite the fact that the Latin that Neville is interested in engaging with is not his own language, his relation to it exhibits his greater capacity to retain the dispositions of his id due to the co-option of its object-cathexes by the super-ego. Language is not so much constitutive or representative of who he is but rather it is what he is predisposed towards. However, maintaining his dispositions at the cost of a more reticent and retiring relationship to language in his ego formation means that even though he might know what he likes he may have a less clear idea of who he is.

For the girls, language is less an object of direct concern but rather a means of articulating the distance from their sense of self they have come to feel. In this sense, they might be considered to be more aware of the repression that school has enforced on their libidinal cathexes. Rhoda regards the 'desks with wells for the ink. We shall write our exercises in ink here. But here I am nobody. I have no face. This great company, all dressed in brown serge, has robbed me of my identity. We are all callous, unfriended.'[17] And for Susan, 'All here is false; all is meretricious.'[18] School has robbed them of their sense of a more libidinally satisfying identity and put them in a context of, often painful, artificiality; the same kind of artificiality the experience of language exhibits for the boys. The two girls' libidinal dispositions make them feel entirely out of place and they are both forced to live this disjunction between id and external experience. Only Jinny seems un-phased by school, concerned more with the colours of dresses she would like to wear and see worn.[19] Later she falls further into concerns that could be related to object-cathexes or its disappointment: 'I hate the small looking-glass on the stairs,' said Jinny. 'It shows our heads only; it cuts off our heads. And my lips are too wide, and my eyes are too close together; I show my gums too much when I laugh.'[20] The language of physicality and appearance is absorbed by her super-ego as she embraces (however self-critically) that which Rhoda and Susan feel alienated by. In the first section of the novel, words make Jinny think of the kinds of dresses she would like to wear,[21] but in this second section she has become entirely disconnected from the written word: 'When I read, a purple rim runs round the black edge of the textbook. Yet I cannot follow any word through its changes. I cannot follow any thought from present to past.'[22] Words that are not directly to do with her sense of self become unintelligible, seemingly through their lack of relevance to her primary concern: her appearance. Where, in the first section, her kiss shattered Louis's experience of primary narcissism, she now exhibits the closest remaining relation to primary narcissistic experience, even if the self-critical voice of the super-ego is ever-present.

Others

The pattern or rhythm of the internal monologues changes once again in the third section. Bernard receives three monologues, interspersed with two from Neville, but Louis, Susan, Rhoda, and Jinny follow in that order with only one each. Bernard's opening sentence sets the introspective tone for this section, focusing on their young adulthood: 'The complexity of things becomes more close,' said Bernard, 'here at college, where the stir and pressure of life are so extreme, where the excitement of mere living becomes daily more urgent. Every hour something new is unburied in the great bran pie. What am I? I ask. This? No, I am that.'[23] The mutability of identity is amplified for Bernard due to his constant reflection on it. Unlike in the previous section where Bernard simply analysed his use of language, here he uses language to address himself:

> *you* understand, *you*, my self, who always comes at a call (that would be a harrowing experience to call and for no one to come; that would make the midnight hollow, and explains the expression of old men in

clubs — they have given up calling for a self who does not come), you understand that I am only superficially represented by what I was saying tonight.[24]

It is not just that he does not know who he is, it is that he is conscious of several selves. Here there are at least two selves, one addressing the other. Despite his confidence as to there being a self who comes at a call, 'something remains floating, unattached.'[25] His identity remains un-unified, scattered, and his education has not helped him to develop his sense of self but has rather contributed to complicating it. A little later in this monologue (or perhaps 'internal' conversation) he attempts to simplify these problems of the pluralisation of the ego by returning to empirical certitude that seems to exemplify the moves of a super-ego: 'When I say to myself, "Bernard", who comes? A faithful, sardonic man, disillusioned, but not embittered. A man of no particular age or calling. Myself, merely. It is he who now takes the poker and rattles the cinders so that they fall in showers through the grate.'[26] Only by absenting the complexity of his ego can he convince himself of his identity, which in itself would entirely invalidate the thought of a more complex psychic economy, bound up in linguistic consciousness. The inability to bring his conscious selves into alignment seems to have no obvious educational solution: there is nothing he can learn which will get him out of this predicament. And, in fact, the more he learns about himself and his experience, the more complicated and unsolvable this problem becomes.

In a very different way Neville also expresses problems of self-knowledge and the inability to learn who he is or who he should be: 'I do not know myself sometimes, or how to measure and name and count out the grains that make me what I am.'[27] However, unlike Bernard, Neville is an eternal student of others, without ever seemingly finding his own voice. While Bernard is caught up in his multiple selves, Neville is defined by his relations to external others, whether they are his friends or writers of great books. On an occasion of a meeting with Bernard he ponders the effect of others on the self (in a manner that succinctly expresses the experience of a Derridean narcissism of the other, that will be introduced in the next chapter):

Something now leaves me; something goes from me to meet that figure who is coming, and assures me that I know him before I see who it is. How curiously one is changed by the addition, even at a distance, of a friend. How useful an office one's friends perform when they recall us. Yet how painful to be recalled, to be mitigated, to have one's self adulterated, mixed up, become part of another. As he approaches I become not myself but Neville mixed with somebody — with whom? — with Bernard? Yes, it is Bernard, and it is to Bernard that I shall put the question, Who am I?[28]

The way in which Neville perceives the affective consequences his friend has on his conception of self indicates that he is in fact aware of something like what, in the following chapter, I go on to describe as the experience of the narcissism of the other. It is not just that he adapts to different settings but that he actually changes: his ego is re-formed in relation. When he engages with a friend he also partly becomes that friend or at least a self somewhat inaugurated by the 'interruption' of that friend. Asking Bernard the question, 'who am I?,' not only implies that Bernard might know him better than he knows himself, but also that he could potentially teach him who he is. However, even though Neville elevates Bernard to the position of a potential educator of his identity (or ego), he is also critical of the way in which Bernard seems to educate himself in his own. His internal monologue directs itself almost accusingly at Bernard and his modelling of his identity on Byron, and reading the poet as a mirror image of himself is itself perhaps another form of self-inauguration:

> You have been reading Byron. You have been marking the passages that seem to approve of your own character. I find marks against all those sentences which seem to express a sardonic yet passionate nature; a moth-like impetuosity dashing itself against hard glass.[29]

This realisation of his friend's imaginative indulgence in exploring the Byronic aspects of his identity leads him to simplify his own understanding of himself. Neville decided not to ask 'who am I?,' but instead insists to himself, perhaps under the influence of the education of what one should believe, inculcated by his super-ego, that 'I am one person – myself. I do not impersonate Catullus, whom I adore.'[30] Even if Neville does not know who he is, he now wants to assure himself that his identity is singular rather than plural, and not malleable. Bernard, on the other hand, becomes more than comfortable with his plurality of selves. Although there is some ambiguity, it seems Neville has got frustrated with him and told him 'You are not Byron; you are your self.' To which Bernard's internal response is 'To be contracted by another person into a single being – how strange.'[31] When Neville leaves him, he feels his 'familiars' return and his plural self restored:

> The mocking, the observant spirits who, even in the crisis and stab of the moment, watched on my behalf now come flocking home again. With their addition, I am Bernard; I am Byron; I am this, that and the other. They darken the air and enrich me, as of old, with their antics, their comments, and cloud the fine simplicity of my moment of emotion. For I am more selves than Neville thinks. We are not simple as our friends would have us to meet their needs.[32]

Bernard has learned to accept his disposition towards plural identity but it is perhaps a quality of his libido which is not easily communicable precisely because it seems to evade the restricting influence of a super-ego. For Neville, Bernard's Byronisms are a façade, whereas for Bernard himself they are a part of a frequently occurring experience of being multiple selves. Bernard knows he is not Byron but he also knows that he is somewhat inaugurated by his writings.

Economy

Louis's experience of his own consciousness and comprehension of his identity is similar to Bernard's in that he does not feel comfortable in the presence of others. However, for him this is because he continues to be extremely self-conscious about certain aspects of his identity, meaning that his relations to others are internally disrupted by the influence of a cruel super-ego, and, of course, the cruel context of social hierarchy to which it responds. For Louis, 'The streamers of my consciousness waver out and are perpetually torn and distressed by their disorder. I cannot therefore concentrate on my dinner.'[33] His disorder is not analogous to Bernard's plurality, nor Neville's reliance on his friends to provide him with his identity. Louis and Jinny are, for very different reasons, the two characters who are most clear about their identities. They do not ponder philosophically about who they are. Louis is entirely clear about the definition of his identity as the son of a banker in Brisbane, who has an Australian accent, and punishes himself psychically for this fact. The affirmation of this identity constantly isolates and undermines him in the world around him. He feels as if his existence is counter to the rhythm of that shared by other people he comes across. While sitting in a café he becomes unsettled by his exclusion:

> Here is the central rhythm; here the common mainspring. I watch it expand, contract; and then expand again. Yet I am not included. If I speak, imitating their accent, they prick their ears, waiting for me to speak again, in order that they may place me – if I come from Canada or Australia, I, who desire above all things to be taken to the arms with love, am alien, external. I, who would wish to feel close over me the protective waves of the ordinary, catch with the tail of my eye some far horizon; am aware of hats bobbing up and down in perpetual disorder.[34]

He defines himself by his externality and therefore in opposition to the world around him. There is very little content to his conception of his own identity, as it is purely a structural relation to a world of which he cannot conceive of himself as being a part. With every social experience, the cruelties of his super-ego are reinforced, to the extent where he relearns his difference and reaffirms his arrhythmic existence. His formal education has not helped him here and neither has the informal education of his ego due to the social hierarchies that have framed the formation of his ego. However, his externality also gifts him with the extraordinary perception of the rhythm of the world, even if he is excluded from it. His sense of its rhythmic perfection both terrifies and attracts him. He longs for the primary narcissistic pleasures that were possible for him in childhood, except he transposes this longing onto the social world in a manner always blocked by his super-ego.

Jinny, like Louis, is also defined by her perception of a kind of rhythm to the world, however, she feels very much included in it. The experience of the self-certainty of her inclusion is clarified by Woolf when Jinny attends a party in London:

> All is exact, prepared. My hair is swept in one curve. My lips are precisely red. I am ready now to join men and women on the stairs, my peers. I pass them, exposed to their gaze, as they are to mine. Like lightning we look but do not soften or show signs of recognition. Our bodies communicate. This is my calling. This is my world.[35]

Her preoccupations are still with appearance and its libidinal satisfactions, which seems to align with the work of her super-ego, allowing her access to the world that Louis and all the other, now, young adults, feel set back from in various ways. For Jinny there is no complex anxieties about her identity or her relations to others. The ease of her libidinal satisfactions can be traced along a line from her early childhood experiences. She is the least conflicted character because the dispositions of her id, even as translated into her super-ego were always predominantly based on object-cathexes rather than submission to an ego ideal. Her education has allowed her to exist in a manner that seems utterly unrepressed.

Rhoda, on the other hand, who also attends the party Jinny is at, is harshly affected by the experience:

> What I say is perpetually contradicted. Each time the door opens I am interrupted. I am not yet twenty-one. I am to be broken. I am to be derided all my life. I am to be cast up and down among these men and women, with their twitching faces, with their lying tongues, like a cork on a rough sea. Like a ribbon of weed I am flung far every time the door opens. I am the foam that sweeps and fills the uttermost rims of the rocks with whiteness; I am also a girl, here in this room.[36]

What Jinny embraces, Rhoda detests. But what Rhoda cannot understand is that Jinny did not make some originary choice to 'fit in,' it was rather predicated by the power of her libidinal object-cathexes from an early age, and which the intentional formal education she was subjected to was not able to overpower, co-opt, or repress. Rhoda cannot be herself in this world and feels at the mercy of it. In the same way that she was unable to grasp the meaning of the words given to her in the classroom in the first section and was left alone to deal with the problem, she is now alone in a crowd, unable to give or find meaning in society and, at the same time, is forced to play by its rules. The analogies she draws between herself and the cork and the ribbon signify the absence of control she conceives herself as being able to assert on the world around her as well as on her own identity and the paths she might wish to take. Her education, like Louis's, has taught her, and arranged her psychic economy in such a way, that she does not fit in and that she should feel bad about that fact.

Woolf seems, in *The Waves*, to chart these demands, accessions, and refusals, within the realm of ego formation itself. We see, at once, how Jinny's dispositionally grounded ability to respond to her libidinal 'calling' allows her to sidestep the provocation of anxiety in a manner the other characters cannot. While Louis, in almost the exact reversal of Jinny's position, defines himself structurally in opposition to, and against the world, as 'alien … external.' Neville, Bernard, and Rhoda, on the other hand, oscillate between these two positions; Neville in his plurality, Bernard with his Byronisms, and Rhoda perhaps, especially, conceiving herself as not of the world but at its mercy. What Woolf helps to illustrate, though, is that the conscious play of our receptivity and refusal is fundamentally produced not only by ego formation but by the broader and much longer standing education of our psychic economy.

Notes

1 A much earlier and less developed version of this chapter, which did not employ any Freudian thought, was published as: Emile Bojesen, 'The Education of Consciousness: Virginia Woolf's *The Waves*,' *Foro de Educación* 16:24 (2018), 99–112.

2 Maureen Chun, 'Between Sensation and Sign: The Secret Language of The Waves,' *Journal of Modern Literature* 36:1 (2012), 55.

3 Maurice Blanchot, *Intro Disaster: Chronicles of Intellectual Life, 1941*, trans. Michael Holland (New York: Fordham University Press, 2014), 133.

4 Ibid., 133.

5 Leo Bersani, *Is the Rectum a Grave? And Other Essays* (Chicago, IL: Chicago University Press, 2010), 110.

6 Virginia Woolf, *The Waves* (Hertfordshire: Wordsworth Classics, 2000), 4.

7 Ibid., 4.

8 Ibid., 5.

9 Ibid., 6.

10 Ibid., 6.

11 Ibid., 10.

12 Ibid., 10.

13 Ibid., 10–11.

14 Ibid., 16.

15 Ibid., 16–17.

16 Ibid., 17.

17 Ibid., 18.

18 Ibid., 17.

19 Ibid., 17.

20 Ibid., 22.
21 Ibid., 10.
22 Ibid., 22.
23 Ibid., 42.
24 Ibid., 42.
25 Ibid., 43.
26 Ibid., 44–45.
27 Ibid., 46.
28 Ibid., 46.
29 Ibid., 48.
30 Ibid., 48.
31 Ibid., 49.
32 Ibid., 49.
33 Ibid., 51.
34 Ibid., 52.
35 Ibid., 56.
36 Ibid., 59.

Chapter 8

Narcissus

Narcissus (and echo)

To even speak of education (rather than experience it without speaking of it) often requires recourse to myth, rhetoric, and the quasi-mythic structures of narrative interpretation. Rather than pretending as if the interpretations of educational experience provided here somehow escape this recourse to myth, they will be explicitly (but also only provisionally) framed with specific reference to the ancient myth of Narcissus (and Ovid's addition of Echo), some of its interpretations, and their rhetorical trajectories. This has already been foreshadowed in my earlier discussion of Woolf's *The Waves* and primary and secondary narcissism in Freud's psychic economy.

The relation necessary to voluntarily sustaining a compulsory education system, and a culture that valorises the relatively specific humanist educational logic that underpins it, might best be interpreted through the quasi-mythic structure of masochism (perhaps partly in relation to Oedipalism), as developed by Freud and many others, directly or indirectly, from Leopold von Sacher-Masoch's *Venus in Furs*. The more general education of a subject, though, can be configured more accurately by another mythic narrative – that of Narcissus and Echo. Many forms of masochism and narcissism overlap in educational experience but as this book is dedicated to examining educational experience that is not primarily determined by a masochistic relation, masochism – as well as the myth of Oedipus, reformulated in the context of Freud's theoretical itinerary as the Oedipus complex – will here take a backseat to narcissism. By turning to the reflections on post-Freudian narcissism by Maurice Blanchot and Jacques Derrida, as well as some of their important interpreters, especially Pleshette DeArmitt (on Derrida), narcissism will be contextualised as an educational phenomenon providing the capacity to exceed and resist the humanist legacy in education.[1]

Blanchot's reading of the myth of Narcissus offers the means for reflection on how the experience of secondary narcissism relates to the experience of education. In conversation with Pascal Possoz, Philippe Lacoue-Labarthe briefly follows a line of thought on Blanchot's Narcissus, claiming 'As for

Narcissus, I'm convinced that what he wanted to destroy is, quite simply, the conventional conception of narcissism. As if Narcissus presupposed a consti- tuted self, looking at itself [...] Instead, Blanchot says that it presupposes it to such a small extent that it is rather a dislocation of the subject even before any possible birth of a subject.'[2] Blanchot attempts to move beyond the common conception of narcissism (where it 'suffices to form the adjective from the noun'), which he suggests can be read, as Freud himself does, in to any posi- tion where the subject finds itself, even if it is found in its dissolution:

> All the positions of being are narcissistic, and of not-being. Even when being is totally renounced – denied to the point of becoming not-being – it does not cease (with the element of ambiguity which then obscures it) to be passively active. Thus the rigors of spiritual purification, even the absolute withdrawal into the void can be seen as narcissistic modes: rela- tively undemanding ways for a disappointed subject, or one uncertain of his identity, to affirm by annulling himself.[3]

This basic secondary narcissism of the subject is unavoidable. In Freudian terms, the formation of the ego necessitates a secondary narcissistic relation produced by its economic relation with the id and the super-ego. Blanchot enhances the Freudian logic, without rejecting it, by arguing that 'the aspect of the myth which Ovid finally forgets is that Narcissus, bending over the spring, does not recognize himself in the fluid image that the water sends back to him.'[4] This would mean that it is not himself he falls in love with but rather 'an image' that is

> not a likeness to anyone or anything: the image characteristically resem- bles nothing. Narcissus falls 'in love' with the image because the image as such – because every image – is attractive: the image exerts the attraction of the void, and of death in its falsity.[5]

Narcissus, then, does not reduce the image to concept, or other to the same. Narcissus does not see himself precisely because he has no concept of what that might be (it must be remembered that he catches his reflec- tion by accident and that he has never seen himself before) and is instead transfixed by the very presentness of *an* image (not of *him*). The immedi- acy of self-revelation is no more present to him than it is for anyone else, and his transfixion by the image is made possible by his inability to con- ceive of himself and construct himself – for example, through language or consciousness – at a distance from experience. As such, the 'teaching of the myth' is, first, that 'a distance is necessary if desire is to be born of not being immediately satisfied.'[6] Thus, rather than representing (second- ary) narcissism as self-regard, the myth posits the danger of not moving beyond primary narcissism and the more direct libidinal satisfactions of what Freud calls object–cathexes. In having his unconscious desire made present, 'Narcissus never began to live.'[7]

Blanchot speculates that Ovid's reasoning for the introduction of the character of the nymph, Echo, into the myth is 'surely in order to tempt us to discover there is a lesson about language which we ourselves add, after the fact.'[8] He elaborates on what this might mean for Narcissus, who

> is supposed to be silent: he has no language save the repetitive sound of a voice which always says to him the self-same thing, and this is a self-sameness which he cannot attribute to himself. And this voice is narcissistic precisely in the sense that he does not love it – in the sense that it gives him nothing *other* to love.[9]

This, then, is not simply another lesson about primary narcissism, nor the demands and limited satisfactions of secondary narcissism, but rather points towards a way out of the narcissistic pride or arrogance of the educated person as installed in and activated by the super-ego. Blanchot distinguishes between vision and voice in a manner analogous to a distinction between education as personal achievement, fulfilling some internalised ideal, and education as an ongoing experience where the ego or self is perpetually formed and reformed, notably through the influence of others in a manner external to resonances with the super-ego and also in perceiving our own voices as, to some extent, voices of an other. Where 'it is vision that exposes men to the peril of the sacred whenever the gaze, through its arrogance quick to scrutinize and to possess, fails to look with restraint and in a retiring mode.'[10] Looking with restraint and in a retiring mode might be the summoning of one's own self-critical voice, where we might convince ourselves that we are less sure of what we are seeing, and its place in our broader understanding, than we think.

Blanchot's interest in looking with restraint and in a retiring mode has much in common with what Nietzsche, in *Twilight of the Idols*, calls 'learning to see,' the practical application of which Nietzsche defines in no uncertain terms: 'one will have become slow, mistrustful, resistant as a *learner* in general.'[11] He provides this definition in the context of outlining 'the three tasks for which educators are required.'

> One has to learn to see, one has to learn to think, one has to learn to speak and write: the end in all three is a noble culture. Learning to see – habituating the eye to repose, to patience, to letting things come to it; learning to defer judgement, to investigate and comprehend the individual case in all its aspects. This is the first preliminary schooling in spirituality: not to react immediately to a stimulus, but to have the restraining, stock-taking instincts in one's control. Learning to see, as I understand it, is almost what is called in unphilosophical language 'strong willpower':

the essence of it is precisely not to 'will,' the ability to defer decision. All unspirituality, all vulgarity, is due to the incapacity to resist a stimulus – one has to react, one obeys every impulse. In many instances, such a compulsion is already morbidity, decline, a symptom of exhaustion – almost everything which unphilosophical crudity designates by the name 'vice' is merely the physiological incapacity not to react. A practical application of having learned to see: one will have to become slow, mistrustful, resistant as a learner in general. In an attitude of hostile calm one will allow the strange, the novel of every kind to approach one first – one will draw one's hand back from it. To stand with all doors open, to prostrate oneself submissively before every petty fact, to be ever itching to mingle with, plunge into other people and other things, in short our celebrated modern 'objectivity,' is bad taste, is ignoble par excellence.[12]

While Nietzsche's idea here could be co-opted under the educational heading of 'critical thinking,' the lesson is not that we learn to better scrutinise what we come across but rather that we become far less sure of our educated capacity to understand those experiences with pre-existing knowledge. It is self-criticality perhaps primarily as the recognition of one's ignorance. On the other hand, though, and unlike Nietzsche, Blanchot is emphatic that what is missing for Narcissus at the pool is in fact an *other* voice. That is to say, a voice that is neither our own voice, launched in a restrained and retiring mode, nor the voice that which either forms or resonates with the educational deference implanted in our super-ego. This other voice inaugurates another narcissism.

The narcissism *of* the other

When, in *Of Grammatology*, Derrida writes that différance is 'the formation of form' and '*on the other hand* the being-imprinted of the imprint,'[13] this could be taken to mean that différance is the condition of the possibility of form or the imprint. However, this condition is no less at work once form has been formed or imprint imprinted because the formation of form (i.e. différance) is not the closure of form but rather the intractable trace of its non-presence and the (im-)possibility of further formation. Différance, like educational experience, broadly conceived, cannot be suspended. As Kas Saghafi notes in his commentary on Derrida's preface to Alain David's *Racisme et Antisemitisme*, a book which, in Saghafi's words, 'highlight[s] all that is at fault with form,'[14] Derrida self-consciously resorts to form to give an account of the book. This 'absurd gesture of repeating the error denounced by David,'[15] that Saghafi encounters, leads him to reflect on that which exceeds form, where the notion of the 'im-possible' becomes important:

> The im-possible would be a relation with the other beyond form, beyond a relation to form, a relation to a figure sans *figure*. This interruption of

form, however, seems to have a *certain* form that exceeds its attributes. Its 'form,' bearing the traces of the unformed, of the amorphous, of a certain nonpresence, puts into crisis all distinction between figure and nonfigure.[16]

To put it in Freudian terms: on the one hand, this interruption of form comes from experience which exceeds a seemingly already constituted psychic economy; on the other hand, it can be read into the initial interruption of primary narcissism as the first stage of the formation of the ego by interrupting the closure of formation that Blanchot locates in the experience of Narcissus at the pool. For Freud, only this latter form of interruption is described as narcissistic, specifically as secondary narcissism. Though, as Blanchot has helped to show, the danger of the closure of a psychic economy, even with a developed ego and super-ego, can also be read into the story of Narcissus and Echo. On a psychological level, the capacity for interruption by other voices is necessary for education. The assumption that one is already sufficiently educated, or more educated than one's interlocutors, contributes to such a closure. The pride or arrogance gifted by the libido in subjection to an ego-ideal, substantially formed by educational means, is itself a product of a secondary narcissistic relation. While primary narcissism dwells with the id, secondary narcissism can partly enclose the entire psychic economy in its subjection to the ego ideal or super-ego.

The demands of fulfilling the externally imposed and internally perpetuated educational demands of the super-ego are sidestepped in Pleshette DeArmitt's reading of Derrida's scattered invocations of narcissism, and their specific relationship to an account of mourning which 'constitutes narcissism,'[17] positing a very different reading where 'for there to be desire at all, for there to be love, it is essential that the other remain sufficiently other so that one still has an interest in making it one's own.'[18] This resonates with a reading of Freud's early papers on children's sexuality by Adam Phillips, who makes the proposal

> that we should all be essentialists trying to be pluralists, and pluralists trying to be essentialists; that we should want to commit ourselves, as persuasively and eloquently as possible, to both sides of the line at once; that we should sustain the conflict inside us and not be trying to resolve it.[19]

Such an ethic can be aligned with Derrida's conception of mourning, which is not limited to the literal mourning of a lost loved one but is instead read into relations with others more generally. Reminiscent of Blanchot's 'lesson about language,' what DeArmitt calls the 'double movement of ex-appropriation' sustains distance and difference and 'prevents the self from closing itself off from the other or from entirely enclosing the other within the self.'[20] DeArmitt clarifies that 'Unlike the psychoanalytic discourses on mourning where an established ego or the identity of the "I" precedes, and consequently can be destabilized by, the ordeal of mourning, Derrida's mourning inaugurates a self.'; 'It is before the gaze of the other – this entirely singular gaze – that I (can) *appear.*'[21] Mourning, in this account, is the (im-)possibility of ex-appropriative relations with others, where a constituted self does not engage with another constituted self, but rather selves inaugurate each other in (non-)relation. With this gesture, DeArmitt helps to show how Derrida punctures the educated power afforded to the super-ego in a relatively closed psychic economy.

The Derridean notion of narcissism articulated by DeArmitt operates at the level of self-appearance and self-inauguration, not within a psychic economy, but rather in its interruption. In addition to formation of form there is also the distinctiveness of a call to come, that exceeds form or figuration. This call is precisely the call for and as the formation of form or the imprinting of the imprint, and is, at the same time, the 'erasure of figurality itself,' in the anticipation or gaze of the figure sans *figure*. The erasure of figurality might then operate in manner similar to the trace, which is, as Derrida writes in 'Différance,' 'not a presence but the simulacrum of a presence that dislocates itself, displaces itself, refers itself, it properly has no site – erasure belongs to its structure.'[22] While Freud's logic of secondary narcissism seemed to suggest the necessity of the super-ego's cruel role in an individual's educational fate, DeArmitt illustrates how Derrida, pre-empted by Blanchot, offers another path for conceiving of narcissism and educational experience. What is particularly important in this reconception within the context of education is that this narcissism does not have to be consciously learned. For both Blanchot and Derrida, this experience is unconditional in human relations, even if the humanist educational legacy, as diagnosed by Freud in the context of psychoanalysis, has done all it can to suppress it and minimise our conception of it *as* education. It is a narcissism against educational authority in the sense that it is not subject to the inculcated external authority manifested by the super-ego. This narcissism is hardly a panacea, though, and it is not difficult to see how it could itself be the means by which certain educational fixations become lodged in the super-ego. However, it also provides a capacity to short-circuit the educational cruelties of a relatively closed psychic economy, or else become the means by which education could be more broadly conceived. In this sense, Derrida's narcissism is at once descriptive and also generative of possible normative approaches to the conceptualisation of educational experience, most importantly, educational experiences that resist imposed authority, and the subsequent pride and arrogance in going about fulfilling or exhibiting its internalised ends.

As DeArmitt shows, Derrida's narcissism 'inaugurates a self.'[23] Such a narcissism is education as self-inauguration and a making responsive or responsible, which is a significant part of what Derrida appreciates in Freud's legacy:

Thanks to the impulse of the initial Freudian send-off [*coup d'envoi*], one can, for example, renew the question of responsibility: in place of a

subject conscious of himself, answering for himself in a sovereign manner before the law, one can introduce the idea of a divided, differentiated
'subject' who cannot be reduced to a conscious, egological intentionality.
And the idea of a 'subject' installing, progressively, laboriously, always
imperfectly, the *stabilized* – this is, nonnatural, essentially and always
unstable – conditions of his or her autonomy: against the inexhaustible
and invincible background of a heteronomy.[24]

This unstable self-inauguration is produced, sustained, and interrupted in
and through non-relation to the other. The self that is inaugurated is, in
DeArmitt's words, 'an ex-appropriating 'self',' that is, an im-possible narcissism.'[25] For Derrida

> ex-appropriation cannot be absolutely stabilized in the form of the sub-
> ject. The subject assumes presence, that is to say sub-stance, stasis, stance.
> Not to be able to stabilize itself *absolutely* would mean to be able *only*
> to be stabilizing itself: relative stabilization of what remains *unstable*, or
> rather *non-stable*. Ex-appropriation no longer closes itself; it never total-
> izes itself.[26]

Equally, ex-appropriation 'implies the irreducibility of the relation to the other.
The other resists all subjectivation, even to the point of the interiorization-
idealization of what one calls the work of mourning.'[27] This is explained in
terms of the singularity of the 'who,' which 'dislocates or divides itself in
gathering itself together to answer to the other, whose call somehow precedes
its own identification with itself, for to this call I can *only* answer, have already
answered, even if I think I am answering "no."'[28] The stabilisation of the subject is an example – the educational example – of the formation of form. Both
subject and form are stabilisable and formable in answer to the other, but they
remain non-stable due to the irreducibility of the relation to the other.

Différance

Is it possible, then, to see the experience of education as resolutely concomitant with stabilisation and formation? When we speak broadly of lifelong
education, for example, does this imply the ongoing stabilisation of the
non-stable subject? Perhaps education is even a stronger term for the specific
stabilisation of the subject, due to the somewhat straightforward assumption
that education necessitates an 'outside' or an 'other' in a manner that stabilisation does not. Such a notion of education, though, would necessitate the
erosion of the typical distinction between activity and passivity. Education is
most commonly, and perhaps almost always, conceived of as being an active,
which is to say, intentional process. It is one thing to emphasise that there is
also what might be called a distinctively passive dimension to education as a

non-agential self-inauguration, but it is another to recognise the passive or non-intentional dimension of education – brought about as and by différance – within what is conceived as active and intentional. For Derrida, 'différance is the name we might give to the "active," moving discord of different forces, and of differences of forces, that Nietzsche sets up against the entire system of metaphysical grammar, wherever this system governs culture, philosophy, and science.'[29] Différance is therefore 'active' in the formation or stabilisation of a passive or non-intentional self-inauguration, in a manner which is set up against the entire system of formal education.

The logic of this narcissism of self-inauguration posits a kind of preliminary secondary narcissism that either immediately inaugurates a self in its responsiveness and/or contributes to or resonates with the already existing secondary narcissistic cathexes displaced from the libido on to the super-ego. Education systems and other cultural and social institutions of community or family life call upon subjects to be formed, or inaugurated through specific means and with intended or even obligatory outcomes that, as Freud might put it, become lodged in the super-ego. Thus, even Derrida's narcissism of self-inauguration is not immune to being co-opted by the dominant educational logic, even if it also exceeds it. The educator (but also the parent, the friend, and so on) is remarkably responsible (certainly in terms of specific cultural inheritances) for the explicit context within which, to a greater or lesser degree, selves are called (upon) to be inaugurated. They are the other to the other. The narcissism of the educator is perceivable in their very self-inauguration as educator; a positional role that is always explicitly relational and non-stable, both in terms of self-inauguration and also in terms of how their calls are received. What is taught, explicitly or implicitly, is not necessarily what is (or all that is) learned.

The claim I would like to advance for this aspect of the educational significance of Derrida's thought relies on its relative inapplicability to educational practice. I say it is inapplicable not because his thinking is not relevant to education but rather because it cannot be taken as a method to be applied. Further, if the ethics of self-inauguration is to be taken seriously, then one of the consequences of this is that what could be called education would seem to occur in more contexts than are commonly conceived. Another consequence is that the traits of 'an' education – whether knowledge, skills, capacities – are structurally non-stable and dependent upon perpetual stabilisation. The other side of this consequence is that a *different* education is possible and even impossible to avoid, that is an education which removes, changes, or replaces (or displaces, dislocates, or refers to) 'an' education already received, or aspects of a self already (non-stably) inaugurated.

The relationship between ego and ego ideal is a secondary narcissistic relation in as much as the super-ego calls for a response and exists on the basis of its own insufficiency, as well as the insufficiency of the ego. In a sense, the experience of the super-ego is, for the psyche, a figuration of the call of the other beyond 'proper' figuration within a relatively closed psychic economy.

By positing the successful identification of a subject with a national or social ideal, and 'educated' (often rather than more material) forms of emancipation, liberation, self-fulfilment, freedom, or some other revelatory outcome that puts the subject in absolute relation to itself and its fulfilled educational experience, difference and otherness are removed from the experience of education. The logic and economy of education becomes a closed shop. The more these educational theories state and practice their 'purpose,' and therefore reach their desired 'outcome,' the less educational they become. This is why these philosophies and practices of education can be understood as being anti-educational. Their basic theoretical structure is that of a fulfilled secondary narcissism, that nonetheless keeps the ego intact. In practice, though, their restrictive structures cannot keep broader educational experience at bay, because, despite their theoretical conceits, conditions of experience cannot be short-circuited. Education keeps on coming. Even theories of intentional education that attempt to produce a very particular kind of educated subject, when put into practice, still educate more broadly, in spite of themselves, because différance cannot be suspended. Formal education, as commonly conceived, is specifically intended to produce stable subjectivities with stable knowledge, not least in terms of ethical and more broadly social relation. What I would call Derrida's narcissism of self-inauguration is education as the formation of form and it can only ever produce or (self-)inaugurate non-stable subjectivities through a narcissistic relation to, for, from, and of the other. In this way, a broader conception of education *is* différance; non-stable but stabilising, narcissistic but *of* the other.

What is required, perhaps, is not only the improvement or transformation of education or even the dissimulation of educational relations in society. Behind the authoritarian practices of education lurks the spectre of our authoritarian psyches and the social relations that uphold and perpetuate their structure. Narcissism of a third kind, not primary or secondary, but of the other, offers a mythico-psychologically framed description of how this might be conceived. For such relations to be possible, education in its current form and conception need not be abandoned; they already occur. However, to become more conscious of the narcissism of the other as an additional form of educational relation might also help in recognising our current restrictive educational economy and its concomitant psychic economy as an abusive transgression of the basic principles underpinning less oppressive human relations. Agreeing with this premise does of course not obviate the ethical responsibility towards those who are currently suffering the consequences of our preposterous educational culture; attempts to make it more bearable and less obstructive to those who suffer most under its weight is a significant task for contemporary educational thinkers, practitioners, activists, and even policy makers. But by the same reasoning, doing so does not mean anyone has to believe the perpetuation of such a system is ultimately for the good. In the same way that anarchists, rightly, do not just protest the legitimacy of the state but also the pernicious social logics which sustain its power, I do not only remonstrate the legitimacy of contemporary educational practices (which is of course wedded to the history of the centralisation of power in the state), I call into question the legitimacy of the entire prevailing logic of education, including its limiting control of psychic economies and educational space.

Notes

1 While the introduction of Leo Bersani's theories of narcissism to an earlier draft of this chapter proved to convolute an already complex argument, I feel it is important to gesture towards their significance in the development of Freud's thought, as well as their applicability to the thinking I have propounded in this book. I hope to take up these ideas in future work.

2 Philippe Lacoue-Labarthe, *Ending and Unending Agony: On Maurice Blanchot,* trans. Hannes Opelz (New York: Fordham University Press, 2015), 106.

3 Maurice Blanchot, *The Writing of the Disaster,* trans. Ann Smock (Lincoln, Nebraska: University of Nebraska Press, 1986), 125.

4 Ibid., 125.

5 Ibid., 125.

6 Ibid., 126.

7 Ibid., 126.

8 Ibid., 127.

9 Ibid., 127.

10 Ibid., 128.

11 Friedrich Nietzsche, *Twilight of the Idols/The Anti-Christ,* trans. R.J. Hollingdale (Harmondsworth: Penguin, 1968), 65.

12 Ibid., 65.

13 Jacques Derrida, *Of Grammatology,* trans. Gayatri Chakravorty Spivak (Baltimore, MD: Johns Hopkins University Press, 1997), 63.

14 Kas Saghafi, *Apparitions – Of Derrida's Other* (New York: Fordham University Press, 2010), 31.

15 Ibid., 31.

16 Ibid., 47–48.

17 Pleshette DeArmitt, *The Right to Narcissism: A Case for Im-Possible Self-Love* (New York: Fordham University Press, 2014), 118.

18 Ibid., 131.

19 Adam Phillips, *The Beast in the Nursery* (London: Faber and Faber, 1998), 33.

20 DeArmitt, *The Right to Narcissism,* 132.

21 Ibid., 120.

22 Jacques Derrida, 'Différance,' in *Margins of Philosophy,* trans. Alan Bass (Brighton: The Harvester Press, 1982), 24.

23 DeArmitt, *The Right to Narcissism,* 120.

24 Jacques Derrida and Elisabeth Roudinesco, *For What Tomorrow: A Dialogue,* trans. Jeff Fort (Stanford, CA: Stanford University Press, 2004), 177.

25 DeArmitt, *The Right to Narcissism,* 140.

26 Jacques Derrida, *Points: Interviews 1974–1994,* trans. Peggy Kamuf et al. (Stanford, CA: Stanford University Press, 1992), 270.

27 Ibid., 270–271.

28 Ibid., 261.

29 Derrida, 'Différance,' 18.

Chapter 9

Space

Architecture

Education is often thought of in two distinct ways, just as often finding itself straddled across both. The first, which is now frequently articulated in a critical manner, is that education *makes* you who you are not already. The second, often more positively framed form, is that education *develops* who you already are; it 'leads out.' Simply defined these are the approaches of constructionist and essentialist (or social and natural) education. The 'value' of education is either perceived as the development of an already existing self or in the capacity of the self to accommodate knowledge and skills which construct it. The binary opposition is quickly overrun by those who emphasise that it is, of course, a combination of both. Educational space, in a broad sense, is then perceived as the space between the natural self and the social world that educates (or miseducates) them in shared values and knowledge that is, through whatever lens, perceived as valuable. In this reading, the self and the social are both knowable and able to be held to account. As such, a totalising educational space is conceived, within which the self is an already existing *potential* to be realised through educational communication with the social, most usually within the context of an educational institution.

As I have argued, educational space is clearly not only present within explicitly educational institutions but can more generally be conceived of as an experiential space of communication. Spaces of institutional education, that is to say, educational buildings (those that make up nurseries, schools, colleges, and universities) formalise this educational space. The act of formalisation is also an act of reduction, to the point that, even if the briefest explication that education occurs in many different places at many different times may be enough to convince someone of its being open-ended, everyday social logic only explicitly designates these specific spaces as educational.

This default definition of educational space can be disrupted. What we tend to understand as educational spaces are imbued with a social logic which clearly demarcates the content and products of educational experience and they therefore come much closer to being imposed spaces of social harmonisation than educational spaces, more broadly speaking. A broader conception of education does not necessarily completely destabilise the subject and can even enforce an already existing perspective or position. Education, in this broader sense, interrupts the subject and brings their insufficiency to light. The reason for articulating this in terms of an alternative conception of educational space is that typical conceptions of educational space perpetuate various predetermined social values, including that of the natural, potential self, to be developed by a linear and progressive humanist logic, lumbered with particular structures of psychic economy and knowledge. The architecture of educational buildings – which is one of the physical manifestations of an imposed theoretical architecture of education – is complicit in this process, its main role being the function it facilitates: a restricted economy of education. The more effective this architecture is at facilitating that anti-educational function the better it is at detracting from the experience of more broadly conceived or specifically interruptive educational experience.

In his entry on 'Architecture' for the Documents Dictionary, Georges Bataille wrote that

> Men seem to represent only an intermediary stage in the morphological process that goes from apes to great edifices. Forms have become ever more static, ever more dominant. Moreover, the human order is bound up from the start with the architectural order, which is nothing but a development of the former. Such that if you attack architecture, whose monumental productions are now the true masters all across the land, gathering the servile multitudes in their shadow, enforcing admiration and astonishment, order and constraint, you are in some ways attacking man. A whole worldly activity, without doubt the most brilliant in the intellectual order, currently tends in this direction, denouncing the inadequacy of human predominance: thus, strange though it may seem, when it is a question of a creature as elegant as the human being, a way opens – as indicated by the painters – towards a bestial monstrousness; as if there were no other possibility for escape from the architectural galley.[1]

Bataille is in his final sentence presumably referring to surrealist painters (Dali, Ernst, Magritte) who deprioritise and put into question the human in their paintings. The 'bestial monstrousness' is a glimpse towards an ultimately inconceivable différance, which, as described in the previous chapter, is the condition of educational experience, and is in and beyond 'the human' as well any abstract 'understanding' of experience more generally. Architecture, for Bataille, enforces a social logic of what it means to be human. Its restricted social conception of the human is artificially shutoff from différance, and therefore from a broader conception of educational experience, not only illustrating the presumed totality of a prescribed human social order but perpetuating and enforcing it. Architecture, in Bataille's reading, exhibits the true mastery of the social over the individual, of the social over broader experience. The economic and social values that dominate our culture and educational institutions *institute themselves* as the totality of being and do not easily find their grip loosened.

Insufficiency

For Bataille there exists a 'principle of insufficiency'[2] at the basis of human life, which de-specifies the content, process, and outcome of educational experience and does not rely on the redemption of that experience in the name of an educational ideal. This principle also substitutes for the notion of an educational lack common to the humanist legacy, which engenders the supposed moral necessity of particular and limited forms of education. Bataille's principle of insufficiency, which makes possible all forms of educational experience, regardless of their epistemological and moral content, is primarily encountered through social relations wherein the 'sufficiency of each being is challenged unceasingly by those who surround him. Even a look expressing admiration is attached to me like a doubt.'[3] As a principle, it can be aligned with ways of thinking about individually and socially oriented education, education informed by social norms and expectation, as well as individual psychological motivations. The doubt that seems concomitant with this insufficiency is perhaps most positively read as that which unsettles self-certainty and externally imposed certainty. In terms of 'inner experience,' which is also the title of the book from which these ideas are taken, the principle of insufficiency is that which opens towards the education of psychic economies. A more negative and perhaps anti-educational reading of the principle of insufficiency is to perceive it as a lack of confidence in ourselves, or at least a sense of psychological doubt conditioned by social scrutiny. Affirming this insufficiency might then allow it to be better understood and accounted for in an educational context and therefore help to avoid its more negative implications. The worst of these negative implications, however, might be tied into the very process of over-accounting for insufficiency, or, an attempt to make a sufficient educational response to insufficiency. A hyper-productive 'space' of education therefore closed to différance: a space of 'education' devoid of educational space.

In his book *Against Architecture: The Writings of Georges Bataille*, Denis Hollier writes on architectural metaphors that 'Architecture refers to whatever here is in an edifice that cannot be reduced to building, whatever allows a construction to escape from purely utilitarian concerns, whatever is aesthetic about it.'[4] But the aesthetic, as we have seen, might also play a utilitarian role – the aesthetic form of a school, for example, might be to produce affects useful to what is conceived within its restrictive economy as learning, success, attainment, and so on. The architectural – aesthetic – component of a school's design might well be that which is *most* utilitarian in terms of social education. That Hollier realises this seems clear from his later argument in the same text that

> Architecture begins by saying what society is (indicative mode), it expresses the soul of society and is, consequently, a simple sign of a transcendent reality that, for its part, would be what it is in its own behalf, independent of this image; but behind this descriptive neutrality there appears progressively an active intervention of the symbol in the very field that it expresses. Architecture, formerly the image of social order, now guarantees and even imposes this order. From being a simple symbol it has now become master.[5]

If Hollier and Bataille are right there can be no discrete discourse of architecture which is neutral and meaning free, especially if architecture expresses the very being of a society. It is, perhaps, society's superego. Even if architecture feigns neutrality, it adds to and enforces (although perhaps sometimes shifts) the dominant forms of social being. In terms of education, it is the image and imposition of a future that adheres to the taught and learned desires of present social orders. In this sense the fate of educational architecture is to master, not interrupt. Its 'space' is the rational space of deduction and reduction to the social order rather than the often irrational space of education, which is instantaneous and conditioned by différance. With différance might arrive a certain inhuman monstrosity that a restrictively rational educational space cannot keep out.

One form of education, perhaps the now dominant form in schooling, offers a sense of sufficiency, particularly if it is dogmatic or certain in itself; its only insufficiency being the lack of application or success of an educational agent – whether teacher or pupil – in achieving their goal. Such a system is governed by superficial and ultimately totalising forms of accountability which reduce the educational subject to an accountable or certificated outcome and their harmonisation with society. This system explicitly and purposefully rejects what is implied by a broader conception of education. Other forms of educational experience maintain and develop the doubt provoked by the principle of insufficiency.

As well as existing under the principle of insufficiency the self is also seen as a 'place of communication.'[6] A conscious understanding of insufficiency is itself insufficient and conditioned by experience wherein 'existence is linked to language. Each person imagines, and therefore knows of his existence with the help of words.'[7] Who we are – and are not yet – is caught up with the linguistic context we inherit and develop individually alongside the social, physical and emotional relationships we might have. As such, architecture, particularly educational architecture, becomes involved in the place of communication that is the self. This is particularly the case if, as Peter Eisenman suggests, architecture can be conceptualised as writing.[8] The architecture involved in an educational space would then also be a part of the space of an insufficient self: a space which is then itself in doubt. However, even if architecture can be conceptualised and read as writing, it can also, and is most usually, conceptualised in terms of what Blanchot (via Lefebvre) calls the 'everyday'[9] that we only rarely step away from and put into question. And, as Bataille writes, architecture 'is the expression of the very being of societies.' In his essay, 'The End of the Classical,' Eisenman proposes 'an expansion beyond the limitations presented by the classical model to the realisation of *architecture as an independent discourse*, free of external values – classical or any other – that is, the intersection of the *meaning-free*, the *arbitrary*, and the *timeless* in the artificial.'[10] However, if Bataille and Blanchot are to be believed, architecture cannot fulfil this seemingly neutral role, particularly for those who do not learn to reflect on it or step back from its 'everydayness.'

Passive education

An educational space is not just a space where education happens; it is a space which educates, often passively.[11] It relies on the principle of insufficiency and the conditioning of différance. Indeed, 'Most learning,' as Ivan Illich has it, 'happens casually, and even intentional learning is not the result of planned instruction.'[12] A passive form of education – which might be experienced in classrooms but also much more widely – is best defined alongside Maurice Blanchot's notions of patience, inattention, and passivity. While John Dewey, as we have seen in Chapter 3, defends a community of thought and purpose, and Jacques Rancière's Jacotot prizes attention, Blanchot writes of passive inattention,

> which, beyond any interest or calculation, lets other be other, leaving them outside the sphere of the violence by which they would be caught, grasped, snared, identified, reduced to sameness. This inattention is not the attitude of an I more attentive to self than to others; it distracts me from myself and this distraction strips the 'I,' exposes it to the passion of the utterly passive, where, with the eyes that are open but that look not, I become infinite absence. Then even the affliction that cannot endure to be seen and which vision cannot endure, lets itself be considered, approached, and perhaps calmed. But this inattention remains ambiguous: either scorn so extreme it disdains to appear, or the extreme of discretion, offered to the point of effacement.[13]

This passive inattention is the disposition with which a 'practice' of retiring and restrained educational relations can be thought, where we let other be other and might *efface ourselves* in that relation. Importantly, individuals engaged in such a relation would not be teachers in the ordinary sense of being employed by a school or university, and teaching classes of students. Anyone we meet might be a teacher for us, just as we might be a teacher for them. Passive 'teachers' and 'learners' would be those inclined towards

non-imposing educational relations (sensitive to the reversibility of the narcissism *of* the other) where they themselves are implicated as other and as
'teacher' in others educational experiences. Such an implication is of course
also the inauguration of a responsibility.

Blanchot's definition of master-student relation from the first chapter of
The Infinite Conversation, 'reveals a singular structure of interrelational space.'[14]
This makes it so that

> the distance from student to master is not the same as the distance from
> master to student – and even more, making it so that there is a separation,
> a kind of abyss between the point occupied by the master, point A, and
> the point occupied by the disciple, point B: a separation that will here-
> after be the measure of every other distance and every other time. Let
> us say more precisely that the presence of A introduces for B, but conse-
> quently also for A, a *relation of infinity* between all things, and above all in
> the very speech that assumes this relation. The master is destined, then,
> not to smooth out the field of relations but to upset it, not to facilitate the
> paths of knowledge, but above all to render them not only more difficult,
> but truly impracticable.[15]

It is the relation itself which is, first and foremost, educative, precisely
because it upsets the smoothness of all relations and reveals any and all
paths to knowledge as difficult and impracticable. This educative relation, which overturns master-student relations, is marked by the disposition of passive inattention, and is conditioned by the unknown, or what
Bataille would call 'non-knowledge.'[16] Knowing is always in relation to
the unknown; knowledge is always in relation to non-knowledge. The
relation of the known and unknown between master and student is an
'irrelation,' which is to say, an 'exhorbitant relation' and a 'relation of
infinity.'[17] The unknown that each represents to the other draws them
both towards the infinite and away from certainty. This relation is passive
and not active. It is the individual's existence rather than their activity that
facilitates this relation, which is not commensurable and has no 'common
measure' or 'common denominator.' The individuals in relation are not
reducible to that relation because it is an irrelation: a relationship of this
kind, in Blanchot's terms, is where *they cannot relate to one another except in
their inability to do so*. This relation has an 'index of "curvature" such that
the relations of A to B will never be direct, symmetrical, or reversible, will
not form a whole, and will not take place in a same time; they will be,
then, neither contemporaneous nor commensurable.'[18] The passive relation
between A and B provokes educational experience as an un-purposeful
education towards infinity and the unknown.

A notion that will be developed at length in the following chapter is
that a conversation marked with passive inattention produces an intensity

which exceeds conceptual formulation in terms of its purpose. The outcomes of this necessarily, to some extent, un-purposeful educational experience are unforeseeable. To say that there is always something more that it is possible to learn is banal but the fact that this is the case means little outside of an educational space. It is the educational relation itself, as educational space, which brings out the experience of this learning. One can learn from reading a text without there being any prescribed reason for doing so; conversing without any expected outcome; experimenting with words, sounds, images, technologies, or practices, in such a way as to let the experience itself dictate the educational outcome, where 'the very *interruption* of relations is nothing other than hearing speech and learning to speak.'[19] This dissymmetrical relational context creates a space of intensity where learning is not only possible but provoked. This intensity, 'generally escaping conceptualisation,' is not the lesson itself, it is rather an experience where the 'disastrous attractiveness' of 'exteriority' returns to interiority.[20] This is the disastrous attractiveness of an educational experience where learning is something which cannot be predetermined and cannot be made 'whole.'

In contradistinction to Dewey's focus on the progressive development of communal values associated with thought and purpose, and Rancière's focus on attention, is this more passive form of education. A form of education marked by an inattention that Blanchot finds to be necessary in friendship 'which has passed leaving no trace,'[21] and 'lets other be other,'[22] rather than holding them to account for their attentiveness, or contaminating them and reducing them to the same. Without arguing that it is necessarily always socially preferable, it is possible to suggest that such an experience of education would not always expect or attempt to account for meaning, value, or attention. Education might then also be experienced without purpose or intention: *If it strikes you....if it doesn't....* Such an experience of education might also elicit what Blanchot calls 'the limit experience':

> The limit experience is the response that man encounters when he has decided to put himself radically in question. This decision involving all being expresses the impossibility of ever stopping, whether it be at some consolation or some truth, at the interests or the results of an action, or with the certitudes of knowledge and belief. It is a movement of contestation that traverses all of history, but that at times closes up into a system, at other times pierces the world to find its end in a beyond where man entrusts himself to an absolute term (God, Being, the Good, Eternity, Unity) – and in each case disavows itself. Let us note, however, that this passion of negative thought does not merge with scepticism, or even with the moves of a methodical doubt. It does not humble the one who bears it, does not strike him with powerlessness, does not judge him incapable of accomplishment.[23]

The limit experience is, by definition, not 'everyday' experience but it can put the everyday into question when it occurs. This cannot be the function of compulsory or obligatory education but it can be a function of the experiences we develop in relation to it in terms of an irrational, interruptive, and instantaneous educational space. This limit experience is the experience of a distinct form of education because of the 'putting into question' it provokes. Blanchot's insistence that this experience does not humble, disempower or disadvantage the subject who experiences it might allow a thinking of this form of educational space alongside more socialising forms of education. To put oneself and one's society into question is not necessarily to epistemologically negate and destroy that society but also to become more broadly educated in and through it. When personal, social, or educational presuppositions are put (or come) into question, education occurs: an educational space comes into existence, even if it is only productive of ignorance. Intentional education is existentially poorer without more broadly conceived education; socially motivated education is existentially poorer without a more broadly conceived space of education. If education is only ever the dispensation of already existing social knowledge, with the aim of developing successful social beings, then it is simply an indoctrination into the dominant social order which perceives 'difference' as something to be understood or reduced to the same, at best, helping it to develop and progress. If this is all education is, and all that educational 'architecture' can support, then the peace afforded by a dominant ideology would allow for the most successful 'educational' spaces. The limit experience is then the *experience of space* or even, *the experience of educational space* which interrupts everyday experience, including that which is commonly referred to as education. And interruption occurs because there is différance.

For Blanchot, interruption is that which facilitates conversation by rupturing perceived totality, such as the perceived totality of an 'educational' space. Conversation – which will be explored in detail in the following chapter but outlined here in terms of educational space – is a marker of différance, not because it involves two or more different voices but because it opens towards something which does not yet exist and, unlike overly structured educational practice, cannot be predetermined, even by an authority. In Blanchot's sense it would also be more than possible to have a conversation with oneself (as he frequently does in his own texts) and this is perhaps the kind of educational conversation that a broader conception or experience of educational space might provoke. For Blanchot, one speaks 'only to interrupt oneself and to render possible the impossible interruption.'[24] And, although speaking is to 'bring the other back to the same in a search of a mediating speech,' it is first and foremost

> to seek to receive the other as other and the foreign as foreign; to seek *autrui*, therefore, in their irreducible difference, in their difference, in their infinite strangeness, an empty strangeness, and such that only an essential discontinuity can retain the affirmation proper to it.[25]

Conversation can prevent rather than facilitate 'any direct communication and any relation of unity.'[26] Which means spaces of conversation might speak to us, interrupt us, and provoke our sense of insufficiency, as educational spaces.

In Blanchot's reading of Bataille, he asserts that Bataille promotes 'not fearing to affirm interruption and rupture in order to come to the point of proposing and expressing – an infinite task – a truly plural speech.'[27] This experience of plurality would also be the condition of an educational space from the perspective of différance. However, if it is not acknowledged or affirmed, it can be glossed over with the fictions of totality and presence, let alone the impositions of social and economic values, marked by the signs of educational accountability. As I have argued, the blocking of différance with the presuppositions of externally imposed values underpins the logic and architecture of humanist education. Unless they are superficially co-opted to a larger educational project, restrictive educational spaces cannot encourage or affirm disruption, rupture, interruption, doubt, or anything, but perhaps the most damaging sense of insufficiency. Even suggesting that educational spaces should promote or be constituted by such interruptive elements would seem to be ignorant of social requirements. But this book is concerned with existential conditions and their effects, as well as with the thinking of educational space as means of conceiving aspects of education which are not forms of socially indoctrinary ego formation. Affirmation of insufficiency is a mark of différance in educational space and, as such, educational space marked by différance opens itself towards the unknowable and the 'interruption of being,' welcoming 'foreignness' without reducing it to the same.[28]

Différance has no value as such because it is *impossible*; it 'exists' under the mark of a 'principle of insufficiency' and is perhaps only perceivable in terms of value as an interruption of value. The underlying principle of an educational space is that it is insufficient. If it is sufficient then there is no opening towards différance and ultimately nothing can actually *occur*. And an educational space where nothing occurs is not an educational space at all.

Notes

1   Georges Bataille, 'Architecture,' in *Rethinking Architecture: A Reader in Cultural Theory*, ed. Neil Leach (London: Routledge, 1997), 21.
2   Georges Bataille, *Inner Experience*, trans. L. A. Boldt (Albany, New York: State University of New York Press, 1988), 81.
3   Ibid., 82.
4   Denis Hollier, *Against Architecture: The writings of Georges Bataille*, trans. Betsy Wing (London: MIT Press, 1992), 31.
5   Ibid., 47.
6   Bataille. *Inner Experience,* 9.
7   Ibid., 83.
8   Peter Eisenman, *Eisenman Inside Out* (New Haven, CT: Yale University Press, 2004), 163.

9   Maurice Blanchot, *The Infinite Conversation*, trans. Susan Hanson (Minneapolis, MN: University of Minnesota Press, 1993), 238–245.

10 Eisenman, *Eisenman Inside Out*, 160.

11 Small parts of this section of this chapter were published in much less developed form as: Emile Bojesen, 'Passive Education,' *Educational Philosophy and Theory* 50:10 (2018), 928–935.

12 Ivan Illich, *Deschooling Society* (London: Marion Boyars, 1971), 12.

13 Maurice Blanchot, *The Writing of the Disaster*, trans. Ann Smock (Lincoln, NE: University of Nebraska Press, 1986), 53–54.

14 Blanchot, *The Infinite Conversation*, 5.

15 Ibid., 5–6.

16 Georges Bataille, *The Unfinished System of Nonknowledge*, trans. Michelle Kendall and Stuart Kendall (Minneapolis, MN: University of Minnesota Press, 2001).

17 Blanchot, *The Infinite Conversation*, 6–7.

18 Ibid., 6.

19 Ibid., 6.

20 Blanchot, *The Writing of the Disaster*, 56–57.

21 Ibid., 27.

22 Ibid., 53.

23 Blanchot, *The Infinite Conversation*, 203–204

24 Ibid., 79.

25 Ibid., 83.

26 Ibid., 77.

27 Ibid., 82.

28 Ibid., 77.

Chapter 10

Conversation

Entretien

Conversation is commonly conceived of as a casual talk between two or more people.[1] For Maurice Blanchot, conversation does not completely lose this association; however, in his understanding, it is not casual because it is an ethically significant experience where language and the movement of thought take priority, rather than the perspectives, positions, or arguments of particular individuals. It is, for him, an experience wherein thinking about what is said becomes more important than saying what we think. From this perspective, new forms of education and educational research can be thought. In conversation, representation, including self-representation, loses its force. This deprioritisation of the individual's ownership and development of their 'selves' also reduces and exceeds the educational authority and power attributed to dialogue and dialectic, which are often, in effect, alternating monologues. Blanchot's version of conversation (in French, 'entretien' not 'conversation,' which has more serious connotations of 'entertainment' and 'maintenance'; entretien is not a chat) as 'plural speech,'[2] unlike dialogue and dialectic, does not imply that contradicting and contrasting thoughts should be brought to shared consensus or internal resolution. The educational dimension of this form of conversation is not beholden to conceptual synthesis or argumentative progression. Conversation researches – but it does so in a manner related to strangeness rather than the confirmation and expansion of the known. Conversation is the 'movement [...] of turning together towards the infinite of speech,'[3] rather than turning towards one another, in defence of one's propositions, or in order to develop them in the name of growth, accumulation, and production. Conversation 'develops' but in a non-linear and self-contradictory fashion. In doing so, it does not leave its initial propositions intact, distinguishing it from dialectic and dialogue.

The space of conversation has something in common with what Karl Hess, in 1980, described as 'anarchism without hyphens.'[4] In Hess's formulation, anarchism does not impose; it states. It 'does not tell you a thing about how free people will behave or what arrangements they will make. It simply says the people have the capacity to make the arrangements.'[5] Anarchism, for Hess, is only very minimally normative: 'It does not say how to be free. It says only that freedom, liberty, can exist.'[6] Anarchism, then, is not an ideological movement but rather an 'ideological statement' that

> says that all people have a capacity for liberty. It says that all anarchists want liberty. And then it is silent. After the pause of that silence, anarchists then mount the stages of their own communities and history and proclaim their, not anarchism's, ideologies – they say how they, how they as anarchists, will make arrangements, describe events, celebrate life, work.[7]

In a sense, the silence between the ideological statement of anarchism, and then any ideological movement that follows, it makes space for, or perhaps even is, the space of conversation and conversational research where non-prescriptive plural speech can be free so long as it does not assert tenets that necessitate conformity or imply oppression as a means or end. The distinction between conversation and more imperious forms of communication is that it neither demands nor expects conformity. In fact, like the basic premise of anarchism, for Hess, it relies on difference:

> A person who describes a world in which everyone must or should behave in a single way, marching to a single drummer is simply not an anarchist. A person who says they prefer this way, even wishing that all would prefer that way, but who then says that all must decide, may certainly be an anarchist. Probably is.[8]

This is not to say all conversational learners, researchers, and educators must be anarchists, or the reverse, but rather that anarchism (or at least an anarchism without hyphens) shares with Blanchotian conversation a form of freedom that is also a kind of allergy to imposition, enforcement, oppression, domination, or coercion. As with the literal and metaphorical space of Blanchot's conversation, 'Liberty finally is,' for Hess, 'not a box into which people are to be forced. Liberty is a space in which people may live. It does not tell you how they will live. It says, eternally, only that we can.'[9]

The movement of thought

The argument presented in this chapter is not intended to suggest that dialogue and dialectic are invalid forms of education or research. Nor will it be argued that dialogue and dialectic cannot be conceived under the umbrella term 'conversation.' What will be argued is that there is something distinctive about conversation as an educational space and form of education, especially in Blanchot's formulation of conversation as plural speech, that exceeds dialogue and dialectic, and therefore also readings of conversation that align it too closely with those specific forms. Further, it will be argued that Blanchot's notion of conversation as plural speech offers a unique way of conceiving of educational research and of education as research. Unlike dialogical and dialectical conceptions of educational research, it allows for a disestablishment of the subject and the scientific framing of research.[10] Educational research is most usually conceived of as social science research, specifically concerned with accumulation or production of knowledge relating to the growth (or barriers to growth) of individual subjects or groups of subjects. Equally, most philosophical research in education relies on a relatively fixed conception of the subject and knowledge, completely in keeping with the humanist legacy. Research through conversation as plural speech is described in a manner that accounts for educational experience and development which does not reinforce the subject or an initial scientific proposition and its concomitant context. To propose conversation as educational research is not to posit a 'better' mode of scientific research but rather a conception of research that necessarily distorts, delays, and betrays scientific method and the humanist legacy. On the one hand, the description of conversation outlined here is a recognition of educational experience that already occurs, and yet, because of the force that humanistically informed scientific logic imposes on educational thought, it is not commonly conceived as such. On the other hand, it outlines a mode of non-scientific research (which is to say, research that abandons stable conceptions of the subject, knowledge, and the human, suspending their significance) as an alternative mode of thought and form of education. This is partly an attempt to disrupt the received notion that education can only be experienced or understood as a scientific or quasi-scientific process that develops a subject in a linear fashion through the accumulation of knowledge. Research and education is here, through conversation as plural speech, conceived also as the movement of thought. Such an approach is not intended to delegitimate a scientific approach to research and education but rather to suggest that it is not the only approach to or experience of research and education, and also to outline what this alternative might look like and how it might be described.

   Conversation as plural speech is developmental, although not in a manner that can be clearly attributed to a particular subject. The movement of thought as language can express (sometimes contradictory) biases and perspectives, despite not being aligned with a secure and stable subject. The intention of conversational research (through plural speech) is not to develop a subject (although this may occur), it is to develop thought. But to develop thought in this manner requires an understanding of research that exceeds the scientific method. Put simply, conversation as research, which is always in this argument educational research, is the movement of thought, however banal or seemingly insignificant the findings of this process might be. A broader conception of research and education is, then, the idea of both as the movement of thought. This does not proscribe narrower and more specific, individually and socially 'useful' forms of education and research. Nonetheless, it is intended to unsettle their foundations and the shuttering of the breadth of educational experience and possibilities of research by the relentless imposition of scientific method. This is not to take a position *against* scientific method, or more practically 'productive' and explicitly subject forming conceptions of education, especially those at a distance from the humanist legacy. Nor does this argument suggest that the idea of conversation as educational research should or even could replace (or even be completely distinct from) more 'instrumental' forms of education and research, especially those associated, for example, with mētis and authorities of competence. Instead, it is an attempt to describe (although not model) the experience of educational research that is not intended to 'produce' knowledge or form and develop a stable subject. The movement of thought that conversation, as plural speech between non-stable subjects, facilitates does therefore not conform to, and perhaps also problematises the self-certainty of, common conceptions of education and research.

Plural speech

In the chapter of Maurice Blanchot's *The Infinite Conversation* titled, 'Interruption: As on a Riemann surface,' before unpacking and problematising it, he defines conversation ('the most simple description of the most simple conversation') as being 'when two people speak together, they speak not together, but each in turn: one says something, then stops, the other something else (or the same thing), then stops.'[11] The intervals produced by the interruption of the sequences of speech are necessary to allowing those sequences to be 'confirmed, contradicted, or developed.'[12] It is the interval or the pause alone that 'permits speech to be constituted as conversation, and even as speech.'[13] This blurring of the boundary between speech and conversation draws attention to the potential conversational conditions required even for 'the repetition of an imperious monologue,' a violence participated in by 'every head of state.'[14] However, 'Interruption is necessary to any succession of words; intermittence makes their becoming possible, discontinuity ensures the continuity of understanding.'[15] These descriptions help to indicate how dialogue and dialectic have been so readily identified with a simple idea of conversation. If even the imperious monologue of a head of state can fit in to the basic logic of conversation, then it might be little surprise that dialogue and dialectic also find a place. What Blanchot thinks is common to, and problematic in, specifically dialectical interpretations of conversation is that they tend towards unity. For Blanchot, 'the "I" wants to annex the other (identify the other with itself) by making of it its own thing, or by studying it as a thing, or, yet again, in wanting to find in it another myself, whether this be through free recognition or through the instantaneous union of two souls.'[16]

Different from these unifying ideas of communication is the approach that Blanchot formulates for speaking (and writing) which is '*to cease thinking solely with a view to unity*, and to make the relations of words an essentially dissymmetrical field governed by discontinuity.'[17] This would produce a 'non-unifying,' 'non-pontificating speech capable of clearing the two shores separated by the abyss, but without filling in the abyss or reuniting its shores.'[18] Blanchot then further distinguishes between these 'two kinds of experience we have with speech,' wherein the former is 'the speech of the universe, tending towards unity and helping to accomplish the whole; the other, the speech of writing, bears a relation of infinity and strangeness.'[19] This can be analogised with the distinction drawn between the scientific and non-scientific modes of educational research in the introduction to this chapter. Despite this distinction, though, Blanchot goes on to state that 'this decisive difference is nonetheless always ambiguous,' as the silence which permits two people to speak 'is still no more than the alternating pause of the first degree; but in this alternance there may also, already, be at work the interruption by which the unknown announces itself.'[20] With this important sentence, Blanchot suggests that even our most basic forms of communication might be conditioned by 'a relation of infinity and strangeness'; again, showing that these two forms of speech cannot be entirely disentangled. The same holds for scientific and non-scientific educational research, although the former often behaves as if the latter does not exist. For Blanchot, speech 'is between us, it holds itself between, and conversation is approach on the basis of this between-two: an irreducible distance that must be preserved if one wishes to maintain a relation with the unknown that is speech's unique gift.'[21] However, the productivity Blanchot is concerned with is distinct from that which is performed in the Socratic dialogues or dialectic (which remain scientific in the general sense defined above), and is 'not a matter of teaching something or of extracting the truth by going from one interlocutor to another, as did Socrates in order to keep seeking the true through the vicissitudes of an unyielding conversation.'[22]

Against such dialectical and dialogical performances, typical of the humanist legacy in education, Blanchot proposes a situation wherein 'a mutual promise is made that commits the play of thought to a common openness in [a] game in which the players are two speaking beings and through which thought is each time asked to affirm its relation to the unknown.'[23] This game is an attempt to reach an 'infinite affirmation' and there is never 'a question of winning, that is, of arguing or giving proof in view of some truth to be known.'[24] The players become 'momentary respondents to this thought of the unknown' and '[f]orgetting is the master of the game.'[25] Here he claims that

> Rather than dialogue, we should name it plural speech. Plural speech, inasmuch as in its simplicity it is the seeking of an affirmation that, though escaping all negation, neither unifies nor allows itself to be unified but rather always refers to a difference always more tempted to defer. This is a speech that is essentially non-dialectical; it says the absolutely other that can never be reduced to the same or to take a place in the whole.[26]

Blanchot analogises this description of plural speech with a game of dice where each player plays for the other rather than against them, and where there is 'no gain other than *the very possibility of playing*.'[27] Blanchot describes this game, and the plural speech and research concomitant with it as

> A non-personal intimacy from which the particularities of each person cannot be entirely excluded but which, in principle, does not take them into account. Indeed each player may bring his particular existence into play, but as a player he is without particularity, introduced by the game into anonymity and reduced to the abstract truth of the infinite risk that takes from him all determined social reality: without history, without anecdote, himself an unknown through this relation with the unknown wherein he affirms himself, and each time asking (as though it were an implicit rule) that all that is known of him be forgotten, or at least not brought into the game.[28]

Such a game might then be imagined in a much broader context of education and educational research than the classroom. It is a form of research as commitment to the educational component of social relationships which, as a 'limit experience is the response that man encounters when he has decided to put himself radically in question.'[29] While such research might inform explicitly scientific research, its basic structure is non-scientific and non-humanistic, and it also pulls at the seams of the scientific claims made for qualitative or action research. Equally, conversation as educational research requires no formal or institutional context and can be experienced (or 'conducted') anywhere the 'movement [...] of turning together towards the infinite of speech' is possible.[30]

Research

For Blanchot there is a clear association between conversation as plural speech and research. The speech relations 'in which the unknown articulates itself' cannot be 'direct, symmetrical, or reversible, will not form a whole, and will not take place in a same time.'[31] As such, a 'linear language of simple development' or of 'assertion and answer' – '*a language where language itself would not be at stake*' – would be inappropriate for research.[32] In attempting to produce an alternative approach to 'the language of research,' which accounts for the 'demand of discontinuity,' he asks

> How can one speak so that speech is essentially plural? How can the search for a plural speech be affirmed, a speech no longer founded upon equality and inequality, no longer upon predominance and subordination, nor upon reciprocal mutuality, but upon dissymmetry and irreversibility so that, between two instances of speech, a relation of infinity would always be involved as the movement of signification itself?[33]

However, this desire to develop plural speech is itself conditioned by the problem of affirmation, development, and even 'assertion and answer.' As such, it would seem that Blanchot, rather than suggesting that plural speech could exist in the absence of any experience of continuity, proposes an approach to research which heeds the 'demand of discontinuity' that the continuous must (and does already, although often unnoticed) turn to. It is, then, in the context of these reflections on research, that Blanchot's later statement – 'speaking, like writing, engages us in a separating movement, an oscillating and vacillating departure.'[34] – might be understood. The unknown is articulated through the movement of oscillation and vacillation that conditions all speech. What Blanchot draws attention to is not the necessity of a final break from development, as some kind of misguided (un)ethical obligation, but rather to the realisation that development is always conditioned by discontinuity. It is in discontinuity that a more complex and unknown development might be turned to. This is the case even if, in terms of the already existing structures of development, a discontinuous 'development' might be considered unproductive. The reverse might also be true, wherein the discontinuous 'development' is far more productive than a linear development from an original proposition might have been. In this reading, it might not be difficult to see what is meant by his statement that 'Whoever would advance must turn aside. This makes for a curious kind of crab's progress.'[35]

Blanchot returns to similarly educational questions in the chapter 'A rose is a rose…,' where he also stylistically models conversation as educational research.[36] The text is itself presented as the 'development' of a conversation between two interlocutors, parodying and critiquing dialogue and dialectic, while also turning away from them. His two interlocutors (who are both him and also not him) concern themselves with how (inspired by the philosopher, Alain – pen name of Émile Chartier) one might 'learn not to develop' which would 'be a matter of thinking by separate affirmations. Someone says something and goes no further. Without proof, reasoning and logical consequence.'[37] Significantly, through the form of plural speech that his own text sometimes exhibits (in the breaking up of his speech, as if into plural, unnamed interlocutors), Blanchot seems to stand against allowing this approach to overdetermine his thinking, at least in terms of defending reason:

> Generally, when someone says something, he or she relates it (implicitly or not) to an ordered set of words, experiences, and principles. These connections of coherency, this search for a common order, and the methodological progression through which thought transforms itself while remaining the same belong to the exigency of reason. A developed thought is a reasonable thought; it is also, I would add, a political thought, for the generality it strives for is that of the universal State when there will be no more private truth and when everything that exists will submit to a common denominator.[38]

Despite the tone of this proclamation, he follows this by using the speech of another interlocutor to state that this is 'A great and fine exigency. Let us develop our thoughts'; the other responding, 'We will most certainly never say anything against reason, except to provoke it, for it easily falls asleep.'[39] It is through the necessity of the provocation of sleeping reason that aspects of some types of scientific research come into question, and that other forms of research can be outlined. That is to say, forms of research not primarily concerned with growth, accumulation, and production, or 'whose principal merit is to conform to our habits or our cultural ideal.'[40] He goes on to say that 'to learn not to develop is to learn to unmask the cultural and social constraint that is expressed in an indirect yet authoritarian manner through the rules of discursive 'development.'[41] It is an unlearning of received propositions and paths for development that would then not be rehearsed within the rhetoric of cultural and social constraints. Authoritarian rhetoric is, for Blanchot, developed most visibly in a 'sermon or a televised address: we know perfectly well that their "truth" lies not in the least in the ideas that are expressed, but wholly in their oratorical development and gesticulation.'[42]

This latter form of linear development, which keeps everything intact and continuous as it progresses, is not defensible through the logic of reason and is instead protected only by the social context which legitimates it and gives power to its rhetoric. The same might be said for dominant scientific conceptions of education and research as linear development. Blanchot makes the point that '[t]he violence of the unreasonable man who gives himself over to some passion is no more menacing than the violence of the man who wants to be right and wants reason to be his.'[43] To this he opposes 'true thoughts,' which '[f]ar from being statements of authority, scorning proof and requiring blind obedience, true thoughts shun the violence that is inherent in the art of demonstrating and arguing.'[44] It is this latter form of violent development that the crab's progress, associated with the plural speech of research, must refuse, interrupt, and turn away from. This is the case, perhaps especially, in terms of our own 'development.' Blanchot's alternative form of non-linear and self-contradictory 'development' must be approached as a refusal of and interruption to the horizon demarcated by the habits of thought educationally produced within cultural and social constraint:

> True thoughts are thoughts of refusal: refusal of natural thought, of the legal and economic order, which imposes itself like a second nature, and of the spontaneity, without research and without caution, which is merely habitual movement that pretends to be movement that is free. True thoughts question, and to question is to think by interrupting oneself.[45]

Conversation productive of the 'true thought' expected of research, then, is hardly simple spontaneity, but is instead the specific refusal and unworking of the received habits we perform as 'second nature.' To the refusal of natural thought and that of the legal and economic order, there might also be added the natural thought associated with education (including the emphasis given to such processes as 'becoming') and the educational order.

In contrast to the self-contradictory and non-linear 'development' of true thoughts, Blanchot again puts in to question the dialogical and dialectical usurpations of conversation and their self-justification as supposedly 'educational' activity. He describes as 'odious,' 'a room where people are speaking, each one taking a discussion as far as it will go, as though each were alone with his own reasoning and seeking to include everything in its development.'[46] In an attempt to formulate a non-odious relational context, one of Blanchot's interlocutors goes on to describe a conversation he observed between two men, where one would speak of 'some truth he had taken to heart' and 'the other would listen in silence, then when reflection had done its work he would in turn express some proposition, sometimes in almost the same words, albeit slightly differently (more rigorously, more loosely, or more strangely).'[47] He conceives of this as 'the strongest of dialogues,' wherein

> Nothing was developed, opposed or modified; and it was manifest that the first interlocutor learned a great deal, and even infinitely, from his own words repeated – not because they were adhered to and agreed with, but, on the contrary, through the infinite difference. For it is as though what he said in the first person as an 'I' had been expressed anew by him as 'other' [autrui] and as though he had thus been carried into the very unknown of his thought: where his thought, without being altered, became absolutely other.[48]

In Blanchot's description, 'these two men had in a certain sense nothing in common, except the movement (which brought them very close) of turning together towards the infinite of speech, which is the meaning of the word conversation.'[49] Separate from this general definition but specific to this particular illustration of it is the concept and practice of repetition, which is 'the insistence of a questioning that interrogates at various levels, without, however, affirming itself in the terms of a question [...] repeating not in order to cast a spell over speech, but rather to disenchant speech with speech itself, to tone it down rather than stifle it.'[50] In nearing the conclusion to that chapter, and repeated here, nearing conclusion to my own, one of the interlocutors draws attention to their paradoxical (but rhetorically significant) development of the claim that 'true thoughts are not developed,' asking 'Now what have we ourselves done but develop this refusal to develop, thus contradicting it and contradicting ourselves in the very demonstration?,'[51] In response, the other interlocutor states that

> At least this should signal to us that there are no thoughts that do not end up, as they are developed, and even within a rigorous and sequential

logic, by presupposing new postulates that are indispensable to this development and that are nonetheless incompatible (or whose compatibility
cannot be demonstrated) with the initial postulate.[52]

It is, in a sense, the conversation that develops, rather than the thought. Or
else, the thought develops in its movement by being turned away from. This
is again what Blanchot calls a crab's progress and is a mode of thinking which
educates through interrupting oneself by means of conversation.

Conversation, while serving a practical function in the context of education and educational research, also performs a role as an analogy for educational experience more generally. Instead of individualising and linear,
progressive growth metaphors, conversation provides a means of conceptualising a form of education that deprioritises individual linear development in favour of the movement of thought. However, this movement
itself, as educational research, helps to develop individuals' thought in
non-anticipatable directions; directions which interrupt the very thinking
that was to be developed.

Educational experience, even educational research, is broader than that
which is prescribed and confined by scientific, or even more broadly theoretical, method. As well as sometimes seeming to 'produce' knowledge and
form subjects, as in the scientific model, educational research as conversation also destabilises and provisionally abandons knowledge and the subject
through the movement of thought. The argument of this book is ultimately
a proposal for a broader conception of education and educational research
as well as being a description of already occurring experiences that are no
less educational for not conforming to a humanist model of education that
requires a relatively stable conception of 'subject' and 'knowledge.' To think
conversation as a form of education and educational research is also to think
education as more than just growth, accumulation, and production.

Notes

1 Parts of this chapter were published in an earlier, open access form as: Emile
  Bojesen, 'Conversation as Educational Research,' *Educational Philosophy and Theory*,
  51:6 (2019), 650–659.
2 Maurice Blanchot, *The Infinite Conversation*, trans. Susan Hanson (Minneapolis,
  MN: University of Minnesota Press, 1993), 215–217.
3 Ibid., 341.
4 Karl Hess, 'Anarchism Without Hyphens,' in *Markets Not Capitalism: Individualist
  Anarchism against Bosses, Inequality, Corporate Power, and Structural Poverty*, ed. Gary
  Chartier and Charles W. Johnson (London: Minor Compositions, 2011).
5 Ibid., 120.
6 Ibid., 120.
7 Ibid., 120.
8 Ibid., 120.
9 Ibid., 120.

10 For an important example of Blanchot's critical engagement with the human
    sciences see Ibid., 249–252.
11 Ibid., 75.
12 Ibid., 75.
13 Ibid., 75.
14 Ibid., 75.
15 Ibid., 76.
16 Ibid., 77.
17 Ibid., 76.
18 Ibid., 78.
19 Ibid., 78.
20 Ibid., 78.
21 Ibid., 212.
22 Ibid., 213.
23 Ibid., 213.
24 Ibid., 213.
25 Ibid., 214.
26 Ibid., 215.
27 Ibid., 216.
28 Ibid., 217.
29 Ibid., 203.
30 Ibid., 341.
31 Ibid., 6.
32 Ibid., 6.
33 Ibid., 8.
34 Ibid., 28.
35 Ibid., 32.
36 While the remainder of this section attempts outline Blanchot's modelling of con-
    versation as educational research in this chapter of *The Infinite Conversation*, inter-
    ested readers are advised to consult this short text directly to further inform their
    understanding of what this version of conversation, research, and education might
    look like in practice; see Ibid., 339–344.
37 Ibid., 339.
38 Ibid., 339.
39 Ibid., 339.
40 Ibid., 340.
41 Ibid., 339–340.
42 Ibid., 340.
43 Ibid., 340.
44 Ibid., 340.
45 Ibid., 340.
46 Ibid., 340–341.
47 Ibid., 341.
48 Ibid., 341.
49 Ibid., 341.
50 Ibid., 342.
51 Ibid., 344.
52 Ibid., 344.

Conclusion

Deschooling

In 1971, the year after Shulamith Firestone published *The Dialectic of Sex* and Pierre Klossowski published *Living Currency*, Ivan Illich published his most influential book, *Deschooling Society*. In his view an entirely 'new approach to incidental or informal education' should be the basis of 'deschooled society,' rather than relying only on 'new formal mechanisms for the formal acquisition of skills and their educational use.'[1] He explicitly differentiates his vision from one which only looks backwards 'to the forms which learning took in the village or the medieval town.'[2] Instead of the 'concentric circles of meaningful structures' experienced in 'traditional society,' meaning in modern society is to be found 'in many structures to which [individuals are] only marginally related.'[3]

For Illich, the educational revolution should be guided by certain goals involving the liberation of 'access to things by abolishing the control which persons and institutions now exercise over their educational values'; 'the sharing of skills by guaranteeing freedom to teach or exercise them on request'; 'the critical and creative resources of people by returning to individual persons the ability to call and hold meetings'; and 'the individual from the obligation to shape his expectations to the services offered by any established profession.'[4]

These liberatory aims would not be underpinned by 'educators' curricular goals' but rather by a range of educational resources that would 'enable the student to gain access to any educational resource which may help him to define and achieve his own goals.'[5] These would include

1 Reference Services to Educational Objects – which facilitate access to things or processes used for formal learning. Some of these things can be reserved for this purpose, stored in libraries, rental agencies, laboratories, and showrooms like museums and theatres; others can be in daily use in factories, airports, or on farms, but made available to students as apprentices or on off hours.

2 Skill Exchanges – which permit persons to list their skills, the conditions under which they are willing to serve as models for others who want to learn these skills, and the addresses at which they can be reached.

3 Peer-Matching – a communications network which permits persons to describe the learning activity in which they wish to engage, in the hope of finding a partner for the enquiry.

4 Reference Services to Educators-at-Large – who can be listed in a directory giving the addresses and self-descriptions of professionals, para-professionals, and freelancers, along with conditions of access to their services. Such educators, as we will see, could be chosen by polling or consulting their former clients.[6]

While many of these services now exist in various forms, thanks in significant part to the Internet, they have not, as Illich hoped and predicted, become an alternative to schooling and the dominant logic of education inherited through the humanist legacy.[7] While his diagnosis of the ills of education remains valid and, in many ways, complements the reading I have provided in this book, the poverty of his prophetic optimism with regard to schooling's imminent downfall has been revealed by the subsequent decades of educational expansionism and what Matthew Charles calls 'pedagogization.'[8]

My own book has sought to update and expand the critical aspect of Illich's thought, without relying on, or falling for, his optimism. The humanist legacy of educational thought and practice has withstood 50 years of technological advancement, as well as multiple attempts to confront its elitisms, compulsions, repressions, exclusions, and hierarchies; technology and these acts of resistance often being co-opted to its ends. Amid such failure it is notable that critical work in educational thought has rarely, since *Deschooling Society*, taken such a radical position against education as commonly conceived and practiced. It seems necessary, then, to not simply re-launch Illich's radical critique of education, but to supplement it with an attempt to articulate a much broader conception of educational experience, so as to highlight more clearly the absurdity of implicitly but primarily understanding education as a necessarily imposed redemptive means to social progress and harmony.

Conversation is one of the forms of educational experience discussed in this book that comes closest to being a 'practice.' One of its elements might be practiced in thinking through, together, how so many of our educational spaces – even those that are somewhat more progressive – are marked far more profoundly by enforcement, oppression, domination, and coercion than they are by the pursuit of freedom, and are far more productive of 'failure,' depression, inequality, anxiety, and conformity to a damaged and damaging system, than a real and actionable sense of non-oppressive liberty. Where educational outcomes are socially asserted and legally regulated or where culturally privileged authority is able to suppress and delegitimate the knowledge of particular individuals, either because of the status of those individuals or the types of knowledge they hold, conversation might be seen as a powerful alternative. Unlike much radical educational thought and practice, conversation prescribes no particular politics, while also puncturing the politically motivated assertions of authority that much educational practice relies on. Conversation is not just a means to an end, it is a space where we can live and learn, seriously, but at a pace of our making, with our own distinct interests, and in a manner where our forms of knowledge, including our embodied knowledge, contribute to a movement of thought that does not have to be externally validated or approved.

Prescriptions

Jean-François Lyotard's two quite different conversational texts, *Instructions Païennes* (1977) and *Au Juste: Conversations* (1979), published in English as *Lessons in Paganism* and *Just Gaming*, can be read as attempts to challenge the authority of grand narratives, as well as his own authority as author and thinker. *Au Juste*, published the same year as *La condition postmoderne: rapport sur le savoir*, was less directly to do with that text than his earlier book, *Économie Libidinale* (1974). In *Au Juste* he engages Jean-Loup Thébaud in seven days of what they explicitly, in French, call 'conversations,' rather than 'entretien.' These took place between November 1977 and June 1978, making it quite likely that they were conceptualised at the same time as *Lessons in Paganism*, itself a conversational text, though of a different sort. *Lessons in Paganism* has more in common with the Blanchotian conversations contained in *The Infinite Conversation* (1974), notably published in the same year as *Économie Libidinale* (translated as *Libidinal Economy*), in the sense that Lyotard is his 'own' interlocutor, questioning and answering himself in the development of his arguments and positions. Lyotard rarely cites Blanchot in his work, but in *Libidinal Economy* he engages with Blanchot's 1965 essay 'L'inconvenance majeure,' which went on to be retitled (as 'L'insurrection, la folie d'écrire') and reworked for publication in *The Infinite Conversation*. While it might be a stretch to conclude that Lyotard was, in the late 70s, specifically concerned with thinking through and experimenting with the possibilities of Blanchotian conversation (as plural speech), it is nonetheless likely that Lyotard was at the very least aware of it and operating roughly in the same terrain, where monologues are 'unmastered.'[9] This is something he points to on the first day of the conversations with Thébaud.

   Much of the first day is dedicated to analysing and laying out what exactly it is they think they are doing. Thébaud challenges Lyotard's conviction in the unmastery of this conversational practice, where 'the speaker [i.e. the author of *Libidinal Economy*] is dispossessed of his mastery.'[10]

> JLT: It could be said, quite to the contrary, that he redoubles it, that it is an opportunity to be masterful in another way.

JFL: No. Because when one is subjected to questioning in a conversation, one is placed on a ground where one is not at all assured of one's mastery, where one can be completely new, innocent, even stupid.[11]

This form of conversation as unmastery employs the disposition of 'restraint and in a retiring mode,' that Blanchot describes in the context of his discussion of Narcissus in *The Writing of the Disaster*.[12] This mode is generative of a non-passive ethical pluralism, which is manifested in the space it provides for the appearance of alternative thought and action distinct from one's own. In the context of such a conversation, the centre of gravity for meaning, purpose, and authority can oscillate between narratives, rather than having to be consolidated to a single major narrative. The non-passive relation between these narratives means that they are always somewhat *prescriptive*, even if they are not *imposed* prescriptions. It is not a matter only of 'letting be,' but also of dynamic reasoning, judgement, and a proliferation of narratives, that might enter the conversations one has. Prescription without mastery can only be navigated in a context as free as possible from imposition and compulsion. Educational imposition and compulsion, as the first half of this book attempted to show, are not just held up by legislation but by cultural dispositions that are not easily unlearned or displaced.

As Madhu Suri Prakash and Gustavo Esteva show,[13] even pedagogies of emancipation (where emancipation through education is more central than tangible material emancipation) can sometimes assume or imply that they are the means to the emancipation of the student's consciousness from ideological imposition. However, as Lyotard's experiments might themselves be seen to demonstrate, it is the pedagogical space itself that should be the first object of emancipation: beginning with the emancipation of small narratives. To suggest, for example, that emancipated critical consciousness is necessarily a class consciousness (which is then the imposition of one ideology as a means to emancipation from another) can ignore the complex, localised, and individualised relationships to oppression and agency. Equally, pedagogies of emancipation can sometimes emphasise the conscientisation of oppression, and action directly against it, as its main objective, rather than the development of non-hierarchical relationships, which avoid the imposition of authority more generally. Blanchotian and Lyotardian conversation, as forms of educational experience, or even practice, are not primarily concerned with the participation in or usurpation of the contemporary democratic politics of the state. While individuals or groups may find that direct action or democratic participation are what serve them and others best in particular instances and on particular issues, this is not its only or primary pedagogic end. This is because, despite its multiple unmastered prescriptions, it does not, constitutively, have prescribed ends. At most, its pedagogic space is an attempt to prefigure increasingly just and non-hierarchical relations, where provisional prescriptions can be developed and opposed in a manner that does not dialectically negate and/or consume small narratives in the name of a major or 'grand' narrative.

For Lyotard, this is called the 'pagan,' which is

> not a slogan; it is rather a denomination, you see. An appellation for a social universe, since this is what we are talking about. A field for the emitting and transmitting of messages that deal with realities. Messages regulated by different types of 'compass,' and thus positioning several ways of turning reality out. This social universe is formed by a plurality of games without any one of them being able to claim that it can say all the others.[14]

However, Lyotard is not at all blind to the fact that prescription is 'fundamental' to the pagan.

> Just as there is a politics in the Greek city, just as there are decisions to be made by Aristotle's judge, just as the sage has to decide whether to be a father or not, to fall in love or not, and so on. There are always prescriptions; one cannot live without prescriptions. It was Ariston's error to have claimed the opposite. I believe that one of the properties of paganism is to leave prescriptions hanging, that is, they are not derived from an ontology. That seems essential to me.[15]

And so it might become clearer why Lyotard's conversational paganism is at odds with forms of emancipatory pedagogy that are based on an inculcation into a particular materialist understanding of society and relation. The truth of what actions one should take, or how one should be disposed, is not revealed through educational experience; it is tested by it. This is why education does not follow a straight line of linear progress and why the imposition of a particular form of education onto others can never be sufficiently justified. Of course, this does not mean that one should not risk certain impositions in some circumstances but rather than any imposition, even on a small child, and especially if it is to become habitual, should not be without consideration. As this book has argued, cultures permeated by the logic and practices of the humanist educational legacy see many of its impositions as 'gifts' that fill a necessary lack in its subjects. It justifies these impositions not only as being necessary but as being 'good.' Rather than a plurality of prescriptions, which individuals might navigate and variously decide upon, the prescriptions of educational compulsion require accommodation and resignation. For Lyotard, the prescription that "'one ought to be pagan" means "one must maximize as much as possible the multiplication of small narratives.'"[16]

However, these multiple small narratives need not always be in opposition to one another, and can sometimes even offer one another support. In 'Lessons on Paganism,' one of the two interlocutors (two Lyotards? or Lyotard and his imagined critic?) argues that 'It may sometimes be possible to unite or even combine efforts and effects, and to both recount and implement particular narratives, but it goes against reason, and reason is pagan, to totalize them on any lasting basis.'[17] The other interlocutor asks if this position is 'In praise of opportunism?,' to which the other responds: 'Of seizing opportunities. Opportunity is the mistress of those who have no masters, the weapon of those who have no arms, and the strength of the weak, amen.'[18] The conversation concludes with a strikingly clear invocation of intent:

> Destroy narrative monopolies, both as exclusive themes (of parties) and as exclusive pragmatics (exclusive to parties and markets). Take away the privileges the narrator has granted himself. Prove that there is as much power – and not less power – in listening, if you are a narratee, and in acting, if you are the narrated (and let fools believe you are singing the praises of servitude when you do so).[19]

The other interlocutor, perhaps bringing to mind prominent descriptions of the contemporary 'neoliberal' subject, asks 'Isn't that self-management (*autogestion*)?' To which, in the final statement of text, the other interlocutor responds:

> Not at all. That is the auto-effect run riot: totalitarian power is insinuated into every body, and the meta-narrative of capital is seen as the canonical narrative. We should be struggling to include meta-narratives, theories and doctrines, and especially political doctrines, in narratives. The intelligentsia's function should not be to tell the truth and save the world, but to will the power to play out, listen to and tell stories. That power is so universal that it would be impossible to deprive the people of it without then answering back. If you want an authority, that is the only place you will find it. Justice means willing it.[20]

Conversation destroys narrative monopolies without voiding the capacity and need for prescription. It relies on a space where contrary and sometimes also oppositional narratives can co-exist, challenging and listening to one another. Sometimes, though, these narratives might become aligned, when a particular opportunity arises or is seized. It de-centres any 'educator' but does not ignore the possibility that they may have a contextually and relationally legitimate authority of competence in particular areas. However, this authority, and the broader narratives that might prop it up should not be beyond scrutiny.

Conversation does not attempt to develop a particular kind of critical subject, although it might name a particular way of understanding and engaging in what Lyotard calls a 'social universe.'[21] As such, conversation can be seen as, on the one hand, being productive of what Blanchot describes as a 'rupture with the powers that be, thus with the notion of power, thus with all places where power predominates,' which would include 'the University, for the idea of knowledge, for the relation determined by a speech that teaches, that leads, and perhaps for all speech.'[22] While, on the other hand, it also has something in common with Leo Bersani's description of teaching, which is, for him,

> a sustained time and space where you do nothing but see how a group of people are going to connect. It's really extraordinary in that way. In teaching, a certain type of group-work can be done, which might slowly disseminate into a fairly significant part of society. It would be a matter of how modes of connectedness subtly change within society.[23]

It would be too easy, though, to read Bersani's observation right back in to the classroom and see it as being possible within the restrictive educational economy that currently exists. While such more broadly educational spaces can of course exist within and alongside this restrictive economy, the risk is that this fact softens or forgives its repressions. Worse, it might be proposed that the broadened conception of education that I have argued for in this book might be adapted to the contemporary classroom, in the name of its improvement.

Against and outside

While, on the one hand, it might be suggested that because the restrictive educational economy exists at the scale it does, and continues to grow, it is utterly unproductive to propose its disavowal rather than its modification. On the other hand, if very few people ever make the argument that the entire logic and practice of education in keeping with the humanist legacy is absurd, damaging, and, in spite of itself, unproductive, then a sustained critical position will have no ground on which to develop.

The first part of this book provided the critical foundations on which a more affirmative conception of educational might be developed, Chapters 1 and 3 showing how even many prominent anarchist thinkers (as well as Jacques Rancière) domesticated their radical social perspectives when it came to educational thought and practice, choosing to opt for compulsory forms of education not at all removed from the principles of the humanist legacy and its more obvious proponents, such as John Dewey. With the help of Leo Bersani, André Gide, and Søren Kierkegaard, Chapter 2 began to outline how many forms of educational experience – those, for example, considered to be unsociable in various ways – exceed the redemptive grasp of the restrictive educational economy, despite that evasion acting as a resource for the logic of progression – figured in that chapter by Dewey and Immanuel Kant – underpinning the humanist legacy. The list of those who have explicitly renounced education, as it is commonly understood, is short, even if it extends beyond those whose thought I have explored here: Charles Fourier, Max Stirner, James Guillaume, Shulamith Firestone, Ivan Illich, Gustavo Esteva, Madhu Prakash, and Ansgar Allen. I have attempted to show, primarily in Chapters 4, 5, and 8–10, and this conclusion, how Maurice Blanchot, Jacques Derrida, Georges Bataille, Pierre Klossowski, Gilles Deleuze, and Jean-François Lyotard, even if they did not or would not have aligned themselves with it, might also lend something to this position, especially in terms of how to think educational experience outside the strictures of the humanist legacy.

The process I initiated in the second part of the book, with Sigmund Freud and Virginia Woolf considered how the psychic economy that Freud described is itself complicit with, and a symptom of, the humanist educational legacy and, as such, might be reconfigured with the help of a broader conception of educational experience, so as to lessen and avoid its repressions. Even if the language of educational experience I went on to develop in defining education as the (de)formation of the non-stable subject (self-inauguration through a narcissism of the other; educational space; passive education; and, conversation) is indebted to that of Maurice Blanchot, Georges Bataille, Jacques Derrida, and Jean-François Lyotard, it is Virginia Woolf's *The Waves* that I consider to be the centrepiece of my argument. Although I have lumbered my reading of Woolf's novel with the job of helping to expand the reach and nuance of Freud's psychic economy in terms of educational experience, it is, as yet, the single richest resource I have found in communicating the breadth of educational experience that both challenges and exceeds the educational authority of the humanist legacy.

Notes

1 Ivan Illich, *Deschooling Society* (London: Marion Boyars, 1971), 22.
2 Ibid., 22.
3 Ibid., 22.
4 Ibid., 103.
5 Ibid., 78.
6 Ibid., 78–79.
7 Ibid., 102.
8 Private conversation but also mentioned here: Matthew Charles, '*Gemeinspruch*: On Transdisciplinarity in Education Theory,' *Radical Philosophy* 183 (2014), 61.
9 Jean-François Lyotard and Jean-Loup Thébaud, *Just Gaming*, trans. Brian Massumi (Manchester: Manchester University Press, 1985), 7.
10 Ibid., 7.
11 Ibid., 7.
12 Maurice Blanchot, *The Writing of the Disaster*, trans. Ann Smock (Lincoln, NE: University of Nebraska Press, 1986), 128.
13 Madhu Suri Prakash and Gustavo Esteva, *Escaping Education: Living and Learning within Grassroots Cultures* (New York: Peter Lang, 2008.
14 Lyotard and Thébaud, *Just Gaming*, 58.

15 Ibid., 59.
16 Ibid., 59.
17 Jean-François Lyotard, 'Lessons in Paganism,' in *The Lyotard Reader*, ed. Andrew Benjamin (Oxford: Blackwell, 1992), 152.
18 Ibid., 152.
19 Ibid., 153.
20 Ibid., 153.
21 Lyotard and Thébaud, *Just Gaming*, 58.
22 Maurice Blanchot, *Political Writings, 1953–1993*, trans. Zakir Paul (New York: Fordham University Press, 2010), 88.
23 Leo Bersani, *Is the Rectum a Grave? And other essays* (Chicago, IL: Chicago University Press, 2010), 200.

Bibliography

Adorno, Theodor. *Aesthetic Theory*. Translated by R. Hullot-Kentor. Minneapolis, MN: University of Minneapolis Press, 1997.

Allen, Ansgar. *The Cynical Educator*. Leicester: Mayfly, 2017.

Allen, Ansgar, and Roy Goddard. *Education and Philosophy: An Introduction*. London: Sage, 2017.

Ariès, Philippe. *Centuries of Childhood*. Translated by Robert Baldick. London: Pimlico, 1996.

Avrich, Paul. *The Modern School Movement: Anarchism and Education in the United States*. Chico, CA: AK Press, 2006.

Bakunin, Mikhail. *The Political Philosophy of Bakunin: Scientific Anarchism*. Edited by G. P. Maximoff. London: The Free Press, 1953.

Bataille, Georges. *The Accursed Share: Volume 1*. Translated by Robert Hurley. New York: Zone Books, 1991.

Bataille, Georges. 'Architecture.' In *Rethinking Architecture: A Reader in Cultural Theory*. Edited by Neil Leach. London: Routledge, 1997.

Bataille, Georges. *Inner Experience*. Translated by L. A. Boldt. Albany, New York: State University of New York Press, 1988.

Bataille, Georges, ed. 'The Notion of Expenditure.' In *Visions of Excess: Selected Writings, 1927–1939*. Translated by Allan Stoekl. Minneapolis, MN: University of Minnesota Press, 1985.

Bataille, Georges. *The Unfinished System of Nonknowledge*. Translated by Michelle Kendall, and Stuart Kendall. Minneapolis, MN: University of Minnesota Press, 2001.

Bersani, Leo. *The Culture of Redemption*. Cambridge, MA: Harvard University Press, 1990.

Bersani, Leo. *The Freudian Body*. New York, NY: Columbia University Press, 1986.

Bersani, Leo. *Is the Rectum a Grave? And Other Essays*. Chicago, IL: Chicago University Press, 2010.

Blanchot, Maurice, ed. 'The Great Reducers.' In *Friendship*. Translated by Elizabeth Rottenberg. Stanford, CA: Stanford University Press, 1997.

Blanchot, Maurice. *The Infinite Conversation*. Translated by Susan Hanson. Minneapolis, MN: University of Minnesota Press, 1993.

Blanchot, Maurice. *Intro Disaster: Chronicles of Intellectual Life, 1941*. Translated by Michael Holland. New York: Fordham University Press, 2014.

Blanchot, Maurice. *Political Writings, 1953–1993*. Translated by Zakir Paul. New York: Fordham University Press, 2010.

Blanchot, Maurice. *Vicious Circles: Two Fictions and 'After the Fact'*. Translated by Paul Auster. Barrytown, NY: Station Hill Press, 1985.

Blanchot, Maurice. *The Writing of the Disaster*. Translated by Ann Smock. Lincoln, NE: University of Nebraska Press, 1986.

Bourdieu, Pierre, and Jean-Claude Passeron. *Reproduction in Education, Society and Culture*. Translated by Richard Nice. London: Sage, 1990.

Calvino, Italo. *The Literature Machine*. Translated by Patrick Creagh. London: Vintage, 1997.

Carr, Wilfred. 'Philosophy and Education—A Symposium.' *Journal of Philosophy of Education* 39, no. 4 (2005).

Cavarero, Adriana. *Inclinations: A Critique of Rectitude*. Translated by Amanda, Minervini, and Adam Sitze. Stanford, CA: Stanford University Press, 2016.

Charles, Matthew. '*Gemeinspruch*: On Transdisciplinarity in Education Theory.' *Radical Philosophy* 183, (2014).

Chun, Maureen. 'Between Sensation and Sign: The Secret Language of the Waves.' *Journal of Modern Literature*, 36, no. 1 (2012).

Cicero. *De Inventione*. Translated by H. M. Hubbell. Cambridge, MA: Harvard University Press, 1949.

Cicero. *De Oratore*. Translated by H. Rackham. Cambridge, MA: Harvard University Press, 1942.

De Man, Paul. *Aesthetic Ideology*. Translated by Andrzej Warminski. Minneapolis, MN: University of Minneapolis Press, 1996.

DeArmitt, Pleshette. *The Right to Narcissism: A Case for Im-Possible Self-Love*. New York: Fordham University Press, 2014.

Deleuze, Gilles. *Bergsonism*. Translated by Hugh, Tomlinson, and Barbara Habberjam. New York: Zone Books, 1991.

Deleuze, Gilles. *Difference and Repetition*. Translated by Paul Patton. London: Continuum, 2004.

Deleuze, Gilles, and Felix Guattari. *Anti-Oedipus: Capitalism and Schizophrenia*. Translated by Robert, Hurley, Mark, Seem, and Helen R. Lane. London: The Athlone Press, 1984.

Derrida, Jacques. 'Différance.' In *Margins of Philosophy*. Translated by Alan Bass. Brighton: The Harvester Press, 1982.

Derrida, Jacques. *Of Grammatology*. Translated by Gayatri Chakravorty Spivak. Baltimore, MD: Johns Hopkins University Press, 1997.

Derrida, Jacques. *Points: Interviews 1974–1994*. Translated by Peggy Kamuf, et al. Stanford, CA: Stanford University Press, 1992.

Derrida, Jacques. *Rogues: Two Essays on Reason*. Translated by Pascale-Anne, Brault, and Michael Nass. Stanford, CA: Stanford University Press, 2004.

Derrida, Jacques. *Who's Afraid of Philosophy?: Right to Philosophy 1*. Translated by Jan Plug. Stanford, CA: Stanford University Press, 2002.

Derrida, Jacques, and Elisabeth Roudinesco. *For What Tomorrow: A Dialogue*. Translated by Jeff Fort. Stanford, CA: Stanford University Press, 2004.

Dewey, John. *Democracy and Education*. London: Macmillan, 1966.

Dewey, John. *How We Think*. Boston, MA: D.C. Heath & Co, 1910.

Dewey, John. *The Political Writings*. Cambridge: Hackett, 1992.

Eisenman, Peter. *Eisenman inside out*. New Haven, CT: Yale University Press, 2004.

Esteva, Gustavo, Dana Lynn Stuchul, and Madhu Suri Prakash. 'From a Pedagogy for Liberation to Liberation from Pedagogy.' In *Rethinking Freire: Globalization and the Environmental Crisis*. Edited by Chet A., Bowers, and Frederique Apffel-Marglin. London: Routledge, 2015.

Firestone, Shulamith. *The Dialectic of Sex*. London: Verso, 2015.

Foucault, Michel. *Discipline and Punish*. Translated by Alan Sheridan. London: Penguin, 1991.

Fourier, Charles. *The Theory of the Four Movements*. Translated by Ian Patterson. Cambridge: Cambridge University Press, 1996.

Freud, Sigmund, ed. 'The Ego and the Id.' In *On Metapsychology*. Harmondsworth: Penguin, 1991.

Freud, Sigmund, ed. 'Moses and Monotheism.' In *The Origins of Religion*. Harmondsworth: Penguin, 1985.

Freud, Sigmund, ed. 'On Narcissism.' In *On Metapsychology*. Harmondsworth: Penguin, 1991.

Gelderloos, Peter. *Anarchy Works: Examples of Anarchist Ideas in Practice*. London: što čitaš, 2018.

Gelderloos, Peter. *Worshipping Power: An Anarchist View of Early State Formation*. Chico, CA: AK Press, 2016.

Gide, André. *The Counterfeiters*. Translated by Dorothy Bussy. Harmondsworth: Penguin, 1966.

Gide, André. *If It Die*. Translated by Dorothy Bussy. Harmondsworth: Penguin, 1977.

Graeber, David. *Fragments of an Anarchist Anthropology*. Chicago, IL: Prickly Paradigm Press, 2004.

Grafton, Anthony, and Lisa Jardine. *From Humanism to the Humanities*. Cambridge, MA: Harvard University Press, 1986.

Graham, Robert. *We Do Not Fear Anarchy We Invoke It: The First International and the Origins of the Anarchist Movement*. Chico, CA: AK Press, 2015.

Guillaume, James. 'On Building the New Social Order.' In *Bakunin on Anarchism*. Edited and translated by Sam Dolgoff. London: Black Rose Books, 2002.

Haddad, Samir. *Derrida and the Inheritance of Democracy*. Bloomington, IN: Indiana University Press, 2013.

Hess, Karl. 'Anarchism Without Hyphens.' In *Markets Not Capitalism: Individualist Anarchism against Bosses, Inequality, Corporate Power, and Structural Poverty*. Edited by Gary, Chartier, and Charles W. Johnson. London: Minor Compositions, 2011.

Hollier, Denis. *Against Architecture: The Writings of Georges Bataille*. Translated by Betsy Wing. London: MIT Press, 1992.

Hunter, Ian. *Culture and Government*. Basingstoke: Macmillan, 1988.

Hunter, Ian. *Rethinking the School*. St Leonard's: Allen and Unwin, 1994.

Illich, Ivan. *Deschooling Society*. London: Marion Boyars, 1971.

Illich, Ivan, ed. 'In Lieu of Education.' In *Towards a History of Needs*. New York: Harper & Row, 1978.

Kant, Immanuel. 'Idea for a Universal History with a Cosmopolitan Intent.' In *Perpetual Peace and Other Essays*. Translated by T. Humphrey. Cambridge: Hackett, 1983.

Kelly, Donald R. *Renaissance Humanism*. Boston, MA: Twayne Publishers, 1991.

Kierkegaard, Søren. *Fear and Trembling*. Translated by Alasdair Hannay. London: Penguin, 2005.

Klossowski, Pierre, ed. *Living Currency*. Translated by Vernon W., Cisney, Nicolae, Morar, and Daniel W. Smith. London: Bloomsbury, 2017.

Klossowski, Pierre, ed. 'Sade and Fourier.' In *Living Currency*. Translated by Paul Foss-Heimlich. London: Bloomsbury, 2017.

Kofman, Sarah. *Smothered Words*. Translated by Madeleine Dobie. Evanston, IL: Northwestern University Press, 1998.

Kropotkin, Peter. *Direct Struggle Against Capital: A Peter Kropotkin Anthology*. Edited by Iain McKay. Chico, CA: AK Press, 2011.

Lacoue-Labarthe, Philippe. *Ending and Unending Agony: On Maurice Blanchot*. Translated by Hannes Opelz. New York: Fordham University Press, 2015.

Lucey, Michael. *Gide's Bent: Sexuality, Politics, Writing*. Oxford: Oxford University Press, 1995.

Lyotard, Jean-François. *Driftworks*. New York: Semiotext(e), 1984.

Lyotard, Jean-François. 'Lessons in Paganism.' In *The Lyotard Reader*. Edited by Andrew Benjamin. Oxford: Blackwell, 1992.

Lyotard, Jean-François, and Jean-Loup Thébaud. *Just Gaming*. Translated by Brian Massumi. Manchester: Manchester University Press, 1985.

Medina, José. *The Epistemology of Resistance: Gender and Racial Oppression, Epistemic Injustice, and Resistant Imaginations*. Oxford: Oxford University Press, 2013.

Nietzsche, Friedrich. *Thus Spoke Zarathustra*. Translated by Adrian Del Caro. Cambridge: Cambridge University Press, 2006.

Nietzsche, Friedrich. *Twilight of the Idols / The Anti-Christ*. Translated by R. J. Hollingdale. Harmondsworth: Penguin, 1968.

Orme, Nicholas. *Medieval Children*. New Haven, CT: Yale University Press, 2001.

Phillips, Adam. *The Beast in the Nursery*. London: Faber and Faber, 1998.

Plato. *Republic* in Plato. *Complete Works*, Edited by J. M. Cooper. Cambridge: Hackett, 1997.

Prakash, Madhu Suri, and Gustavo Esteva. *Escaping Education: Living and Learning Within Grassroots Cultures*. New York: Peter Lang, 2008.

Proudhon, Pierre-Joseph. *Property is Theft!: A Pierre-Joseph Proudhon Anthology*. Edited by Iain McKay. Chico, CA: AK Press, 2011.

Quintilian. *Institutio Oratoria*. Translated by Donald A. Russell. Cambridge, MA: Harvard University Press, 2001.

Rancière, Jacques. *The Ignorant Schoolmaster: Five Lessons in Intellectual Emancipation*. Translated by Kristin Ross. Stanford, CA: Stanford University Press, 1991.

Read, Herbert. *Education Through Art*. London: Faber and Faber, 1958.

Read, Herbert. 'The Philosophy of Anarchism', *The Anarchist Library*. https://theanarchistlibrary.org/library/herbert-read-the-philosophy-of-anarchism. Accessed July 11, 2019.

Rothbard, Murray. *Education: Free and Compulsory*. Auburn, AL: Ludwig von Mises Institute, 1999.

Saghafi, Kas. *Apparitions – Of Derrida's Other*. New York: Fordham University Press, 2010.

Schiller, Friedrich. *On the Aesthetic Education of Man*. Translated by R. Snell. New York: Dover, 2004.

Scott, James C. *Seeing Like a State: How Certain Schemes to Improve the Human Condition Have Failed*. New Haven, CT: Yale University Press, 1998.

Stirner, Max. 'The False Principle of Our Education or, Humanism and Realism.' *The Anarchist Library*. https://theanarchistlibrary.org/library/max-stirner-the-false-principle-of-our-education. Accessed July 11, 2019.

Todd, Margo. *Christian Humanism and the Puritan Order*. Cambridge: Cambridge University Press, 1987.

Ward, Colin. *Anarchy in Action*. Oakland, CA: PM Press, 2018.

Webb, Darren. 'Educational Studies and the Domestication of Utopia.' *British Journal of Educational Studies*, 64, no. 4, (2016).

Woodcock, George, ed. 'The Anarchists: A Bibliographical Supplement.' In *The Anarchist Reader*. Glasgow: Fontana, 1977.

Woolf, Virginia. *The Waves*. Hertfordshire: Wordsworth Classics, 2000.

Acknowledgements

There are a significant number of people who have been supportive in the production of this book, most notable among these are Chris Mounsey and Ansgar Allen, without whom I would never have had the conversations that led me to much of this thinking. I would like to extend my gratitude to them, as well as Sam Sellar, Matthew Charles, Darren Webb, Samir Haddad, and the other members of the Francophone Studies reading group at Fordham University, Thomas Clément Mercier, especially for his insights on entretien, Ryan Tracy, Camilla Stanger, John Brackstone, Matthew Clarke, Laurence Davis, Mario Di Paolantonio, Marie Morgan, Janice de Sousa, Mark Rutter, Sam Ladkin, Bob McKay, Vicky Randall, Apoorva Mathur, Emilie Coin, and Swapnil Joshi. I would also like to acknowledge the support of my friends and family who may not read this book but should know that it could not have been written without them.

Index